WITHDRAWN

D1202419

The Bid Manager's Handbook

For my wife, Suzy, without whose encouragement I probably would not have published anything in the first place.

The Bid Manager's Handbook

DAVID NICKSON

GOWER

Published by
Gower Publishing Limited
Gower House
Croft Road
Aldershot
Hants GU11 3HR
England

Gower Publishing Company
Suite 420
101 Cherry Street
Burlington, VT 05401-4405
USA

British Library Cataloguing in Publication Data
Nickson, David
  The bid manager's handbook
  1. Letting of contracts - Handbooks, manuals, etc.
  2. Proposal writing in business 3. Proposal writing in public contracting
  I. Title
  658.4'04

Library of Congress Control Number: 2002106634

ISBN 0 566 08512 7

Typeset by Bournemouth Colour Press, Parkstone
Printed and bound in Great Britain by MPG Books Ltd, Bodmin, Cornwall

Contents

List of Figures

1 *Introduction*

To be persuasive, we must be believable. To be believable, we must be credible. To be credible, we must be truthful. (Edward R. Murrow)

This book is aimed at anyone who has to write, manage, or contribute to a bid for new or repeat business in any context. If you have picked up this book, this probably means you! In most corporate, as well as smaller-sized businesses, government/non-governmental agencies and charitable organizations bidding for new business is a vital activity. The problem is, not everyone gets it right. This book will help you:

- make sure that you know what needs to be done;
- know how to present the information to the prospective client effectively;
- identify the skills that are needed to get the job done.

Even more importantly it will show you how to save time, the most important commodity in any bid as it is always in short supply.

Bids occur in all market sectors, both public and private. The chances of anyone working for more than a few years in any arena without being involved in a bid of some form are

Figure 1.1 *Mind Map®: Bid management*

relatively small. So although this book is targeted at those who have to manage bids, it also contains useful information for anyone working on a bid.

The reader is provided with practical help on managing bids, writing contributions for them, supporting them, coping with the impact they have on the organization and surviving them in general. Hints, tips and checklists are backed up with case studies based upon real-life experiences.

The Mind Map® in Figure 1.1 provides an overview of how the book fits together. Each part has been written to work on its own, although some cross-references were inevitable if repetition was to be kept to a minimum.

> *Note.* There are many terms in popular usage for the recipient of a bid – prospect, customer, client, procurer and so on. In this book the term 'client' has been adopted because, regardless of whether the bid is successful or not, you have a working relationship with them.

What is a bid?

> *Definition.* A bid is an approach to a client in order to gain *significant* new or repeat business.

It is also a collection of information, including a price and costs, put together often by a team to support a business case. The bid document can range from a few pages with a little budgetary justification, all the way through to a multi-volume, thousand page plus submission for major government procurements such as Private Public Partnerships (PPP). Similarly, the value of such bids can range from a few thousand pounds through to hundreds of millions of pounds.

What every bid has in common is that it has to be produced within a highly charged and competitive environment, to a fixed timetable and often to a fixed budget. In this book we hope to support the bidding process for the medium to large bids in this range, bids where there is a significant organizational and editorial task to be performed across departments, territories, job functions and even between disparate companies.

Talk to anyone who has worked on a bid and the one thing they always tell you is that, 'there's never enough time'. The primary goal of this book is to enable the reader to make the best use of the time available and work effectively to produce a high-quality bid with the smallest amount of hassle. (Although a bid is defined as the overall process and the proposal as a deliverable, their usage is often interchangeable. The author makes no apology for this.)

> *Key point.* Why is not a bid the same as a project? Because it really does have a fixed timetable and the deliverable is not negotiable. The Bid Manager is there to get the bid out with the resources available to the highest quality possible. There are no rewards for coming in under budget or finishing early. The goal is to support the winning of the business. This makes Bid Managers different from project managers.

Why do we do them?

The short answer is, 'To gain significant new business or funding'. A more considered response is to:

- persuade the client to buy your solution, accept your proposition;
- define the solution you are offering;
- set client expectations of what they will receive;
- determine the price of what you supply;
- limit your liability.

A bid can be an important vehicle for selling a solution, a product, a service, a portfolio of services and products. A successful bid often provides the basis for the contract between the supplier and the client for supply, and therefore takes on a more strategic role for the business.

Bids and proposals are sometimes only part of the selling process. Some companies maintain such a close a relationship with the client that they never have to write a proposal, or, at least, not until long after the sale has gone through!

Good bids and proposals, on their own may not win you business – bad ones, however, will lose it!

In other words a bid/proposal has two principal, and sometimes conflicting, functions, that of a selling tool and a (sometimes legally binding) commitment to supply. This book looks closely at the writing skills needed to help resolve this conflict (see Part 2).

Structure

The book is organized into three main parts.

1   Bid management;
2   Writing and editorial;
3   Personal skills.

Each part addresses the key aspects of bid management and, as stated earlier, can be used separately to meet the requirements of different readers.

'Bid management' is concerned with the what, where and when of bids in general and in particular. 'Writing and editorial' deals with how to put across a strong message in writing, how to deal with the requirement to address multiple audiences within the one document, and how to produce a consistent proposal from a multiplicity of sources. The last part, 'Personal skills', deals with the abilities that a Bid Manager will need to have to cope with the human aspects of running a bid, for example managing the bid team, negotiating for resources, communicating sales themes, etc. Each chapter contains case studies to illustrate the point and, where appropriate, checklists for the Bid Manager's use. These checklists are also presented in a collated form on separate pages at the end of the book. These can then be photocopied for repeated use on new bids and proposals.

The parts are themselves structured as follows:

Part 1 Bid Management

Roles and responsibilities	What a Bid Manager does – common variations in scope for different organizations. Job description, bid teams and interface with sales.
Methods and approaches	Strategies for running bids, keeping it quick and adaptable. Use of a bid brief and reviews to produce high-quality product.
Risk	Risk management for Bid Managers. Sources of risk, impact and probability. Effect of change. Documentation.
Administration and logistics	Bid files and bid briefs, documenting who does what, progress checking without tears. Documentation and meetings, use of technology, staff and facilities.
Planning	Sample plans, flexibility vs the need to keep control, what activities you need to allow for – how long do some things really take? Resources and activities, typical deliverables, cost of bidding.

Part 2 Writing and Editorial

Writing skills	Aimed at bid/proposal authors and contributors to the bids, helping technical and specialist writers to cope with non-specialist audiences. Style, matching to audience. Fact, feature, benefit. Letters and emails, writing management summaries.
Editorial skills	Pulling together differing styles, matching styles to readers. Use of templates, style, spelling and grammar, tracking progress.
Layout and presentation	What you should/should not have on the page – basics of presenting information. Sample layouts, binders, covers and spines, presentations and style guides.

Part 3 Personal Skills

Communication	Communications strategies and tactics for Bid Managers, communicating messages to the team and the client. Presentations, different media, what works and what does not. Meetings and facilitation.
Teams	How to get people to work together, what goes wrong and how to put it right, working under pressure. Being aware of the organization and its behaviours, tailoring your approach to fit in with this. Conflicts and communication within teams. Composition of bid teams. Dealing with subcontractors.
Negotiation	Negotiation within your organization and with the client. Negotiation cycle. Practical strategies, choosing the right one. What are the negotiable items available to the Bid Manager?
Sales	Qualification of bids, sales awareness, practical techniques such as SWOT analysis. Understanding how sales strategy impacts on bids, what is typical in strategies for major procurements, reasons for bidding, loss leaders, market presence, etc. Awareness of how the client, third parties and the culture of the bidder's organization may affect each other.

Finally there is the Appendix containing a sample bid brief template, a glossary of bid related terms and some suggested further reading.

1 *Bid Management*

Part 1: Summary

Part 1 covers all the different tasks and activities that a Bid Manager might need to do in order to fulfil the varying roles that may be encountered in different organizations (see Figure P.1). Even if you, as Bid Manager, do not find yourself tasked with all of these, you need to make sure that the remainder are being completed by someone else, otherwise there is a good chance that the bid will not be produced, or that there will be some nasty surprises towards the end. The checklists will help the reader make sure that nothing has been missed. They will also act as an aide-memoire as the bid progresses and provide the basis for defining the roles and responsibilities of the Bid Manager.

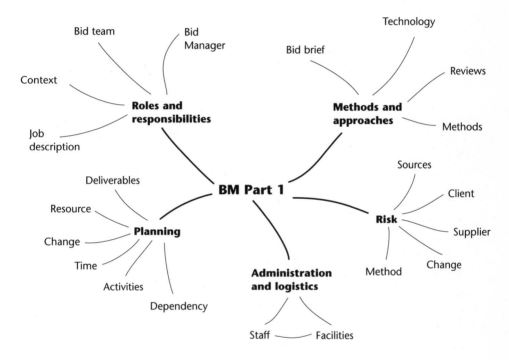

Figure P.1   *Mind Map®: Bid management, Part 1*

2 *Roles and Responsibilities*

Responsibility, n. A detachable burden easily shifted to the shoulders of God, Fate, Fortune or one's neighbor. (Ambrose Bierce 1881–1911)

What is a Bid Manager, and what does the job entail? Looking at the roles and responsibilities that apply to a Bid Manager, or the person nominated to deliver a bid, provides the answer to this question (see Figure 2.1). The first thing to note is that this will vary from organization to organization and depend to some extent on the background and skill set of the person involved. One of the goals of this chapter is to provide a model for producing a job description for a Bid Manager for organizations that do not already have one.

In order to set about this, the context of the role of the Bid Manager will be defined so that it becomes clear where a Bid Manager fits in, irrespective of the details of the specific bid.

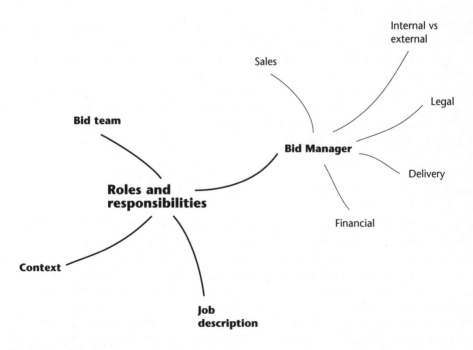

Figure 2.1　*Mind Map®: Roles and responsibilities*

Why have roles and responsibilities?

There is a very strong case that everyone should have their roles and responsibilities defined, typically in the form of terms of reference. People need to know what they are supposed to be doing, whom they should report to and who reports to them in order to do their job. The importance of this varies from job to job, and the requirement for definition needs to be tempered with the need for flexibility. However, for safety and mission-critical roles it is a high-risk strategy not to have such terms of reference.

Bid Managers, by definition, have a role that is critical to winning new business for an organization, vital to continued existence. However, in many instances such bids are 'special events' that do not happen every day. For example, a utilities company may bid for a multi-million pound per year operation and then run it for 10, or even 25 years, before it needs to bid again. The bidding process is going to be rare when compared with day-to-day operation. So, it is more likely that the day-to-day operation will be better understood than the bidding process. Unsurprisingly, experience shows that it is more likely that the familiar processes will be better documented than the unfamiliar ones. Because of this combination of unfamiliarity and criticality it is vital that the role and responsibilities of the Bid Manager, and indeed the entire bid team, are defined. The Bid Manager will often be someone whose main role is to do something else, or is a specialist from outside the organization. Either way there will be a need to define who is going to do what. Without this sound foundation the Bid Manager will struggle to build an effective bid.

Role of the Bid Manager

This varies from organization to organization. Strong evidence for this can be found in the wide range of salaries – at least a four to one ratio – that are offered to Bid Managers. At one end of the scale the job can be largely an administrative and logistical one, at the other it can be a combination of that of a sales, delivery and project manager. Keeping in mind the definition of a bid, 'an approach to a client in order to gain significant new or repeat business', it is the upper reaches of this range that we are concerned with here. The Bid Manager will be a person who has to deliver the bid and in doing so has to manage multiple resources and deal with complex business relationships in supporting the delivery of a strong, winning, sales case to the client.

Context

In order to define the role of the Bid Manager it is necessary to put it in the context of all the other people and departments that are likely to be involved in a bid. One way is to look at the composition of a generic team that could be found in any organization bidding for business or funding. This team may be specially set up for the bid, or may be brought into being 'virtually' as a result of the individuals being called upon to contribute to the bid documents (Figure 2.2).

A better way of looking at this is to consider with whom in other parts of the organization the Bid Manager will need to interact. Figure 2.3 shows how a bid interfaces with a typical organization.

Figure 2.2 *Composition of a generic team*

Figure 2.3 *Bid interfaces in a typical organization*

Bids, by their nature, involve staff from across the whole breadth of an organization. The Bid Manager will need to be able to interact with all these specialists and will need to know what their roles and responsibilities are, and what they can and cannot be asked to deliver, if the job is to be done. The next few subsections look at these resources and suggest what to expect. The Bid Manager's role needs to encompass all these interactions.

BID MANAGERS AND SALES

The overlap between sales and the Bid Manager is one that needs to be very clearly defined from the start if the bid is to run smoothly. It is most important to have the ownership of the sales strategy defined. The author's view is that this should belong firmly with the sales function, though this is by no means always the case. In some organizations Bid Managers come from the legal and commercial department. These tend to be companies where a significant part of the bid work is related to the legal terms and conditions side of the supply. In this case sales become another specialist supplier to the bid.

The following are deliverables that typically require contributions from sales:

Deliverable	Description
Sales strategy	The approach to be taken in order to win the business.
Sales themes	The themes that need to be communicated to the client to support the sales strategy.
Pricing	Conversion of cost and financial options into the price needed to support the sales strategy.

BID MANAGERS AND PROJECT MANAGERS

To some extent all Bid Managers are project managers. As stated a bid has many of the characteristics of a project in that it is a fixed chunk of work with a defined beginning and end point, a specific objective and identified deliverables. For this reason some organizations source their Bid Managers from project managers.

> *Food for thought.* The author is aware of at least one company that has a sales strategy of using project managers as Bid Managers, the concept being that if the business is won then the same project manager carries on to project/services that have been sold. This has the benefit of offering the client continuity and allows the project manager to build a working relationship with the client and to 'hit the ground running' once the deal is signed, reducing delays and so forth. This strategy does work, but it is only applicable where there is a strong project element to the sale and where there is a project manager with the relevant skill set available. Only organizations that are in a project-orientated business are likely to have such people to hand. It also means that any lack of sales skills on the part of the project manager will have to be supplied from elsewhere within the organization.

The more common situation is that there is a project manager whose job is to put together the plans for implementing what is to be sold to the client. In this case there will be an overlap between what the Bid Manager has to do and what the project manager has to do. It is critical that the interface between these two people is well defined. In particular this must be very clear where client deliverables are concerned. For example, the project risk register (as opposed to the bid risk register, see Chapter 4) would normally belong to the project manager. However, it would need to be clearly defined who covered risks coming from non-project elements of the supply to the client. Typically the project manager would be responsible for delivering the project plan for implementing the client's requirements, any documentation on methods and standards that relate to project management, risk plans and any assumptions and constraints that would apply. The project manager would also be a source of cost information.

The following are deliverables that typically require contributions from project managers:

Deliverable	Description
Project plan	Project plan to the level of detail required by the client. In addition a sufficiently detailed internal plan to allow project costs to be estimated as reliably as possible. Estimate of accuracy of any such estimates. Any plans must be in line with any quality standards for project management such as PRINCE 2 (either for the client, supplier or both).
Risk plan	Risk management documentation for the products and services to be supplied to the client, highlight any which also imply risk for the bid.

> *Note.* Who owns the solution? Where there is a bespoke set of products and services to be supplied there needs to be one person who understands how it all fits together. This may be the project manager, it may be the Bid Manager if appropriately skilled. In some companies there is a role called solutions architect or it may be a technical design authority. Whatever the job title, the key point is that someone has to do it, and the Bid Manager needs to know who it is.

BID MANAGERS AND TECHNICAL SPECIALISTS

These specialists will be industry specific. For example in the information technology sector they might include system and database designers, networking specialists, capacity planners and so forth. In the water industry it might include civil engineers, water-processing specialists, hydraulic engineers, architects and the like. These people all have something in common – they are usually specialists in what they do, not in selling it to the client. They will contribute to the design of whatever is to be delivered to the client. The Bid Manager will need to support them in this and make sure they have all the information they need to contribute positively to the bid. Another factor they may have in common is having 'fee-paying' customers to service. Tin this case their priority will tend to be the fee payers, not the sales prospect. It is important to be sensitive to this and to make sure a reasonable compromise can be made.

The following are deliverables that typically require contributions from technical specialists:

Deliverable	Description
Design	Overall technical design of what will be proposed to the client to a level of detail that allows it to be costed and to be evaluated by delivery staff as a viable solution.
Performance	Specifications relating to the performance, capacity, expandability and so forth for the solution proposed for the client.
Equipment requirements	Specifications (in part to support costing) for equipment and plant to be supplied as part of the solution. Any environmental requirements to allow building/premises to be identified.
Development requirements:	
Technical constraints	Any constraints that apply to the solution, particularly any that impact the client directly.
Risk	Identification of any areas of risk that arise from the proposed design; for example, use of leading-edge, untried technology.

BID MANAGERS AND IMPLEMENTERS

The Bid Manager will need to interact with those who are going to end up delivering the products and/or services to the client. This may be to obtain sign-off/approval to the effect that what is being bid can be delivered, or it may be to have them contribute to the bid itself. These people differ from the technical specialists in that they are in the operational, rather than the design side of the business. They may, or may not, have the skills needed to define the solution but they will know what has to be put in place in order to make it work. Again they will have other calls on their time; in fact they are quite likely to have a full-time job with an existing customer so their time will be the hardest to gain. However, experience shows that their input will be highly valued by the client. Demonstrating a clear understanding of what is needed to make the client's business run smoothly will make a very positive impression.

The following are deliverables that typically require contributions from implementers:

Deliverable	Description
Operational solution	Contribution to any operational design, including logistical, staffing, reporting, service levels and other issues.
Cost drivers	Staff and premises required to run the solution after delivery.
Risk	Areas where there is perceived operational risk.

BID MANAGERS AND FINANCE

Here the relationship is usually straightforward. The commercial specialists will normally have both a contributory role and a reviewing role in the production and pricing of the bid.

Finance will be a source of information for any cost modelling and will normally be involved in any financing deals, currency deals, leasing, discounts, margins and so on.

The following are deliverables that typically require contributions from finance:

Deliverable	Description
Payment schedules	Comments and suggestions relating to client proposed schedules for payment, costs associated with them, alternative suggestions for funding and related issues.
Leasing options	Finance deals available to underwrite business or make it easier for the client to afford, more favourable cash flow and so forth.
Cash flow forecasts	Financial modelling of how the business will run once the client has given the go ahead.
Cost information	Raw cost information such as daily rates for staff, cost of office space and services, purchasing equipment and so on.
Credit information	Is client creditworthy, is any subcontractor creditworthy?
Financial reports	Annual report information such as trading profit/loss.

> *Note.* In some organizations the finance and legal departments have a combined function and there may be 'commercial' specialists who will work with a bid team providing both types of advice.

BID MANAGERS AND LEGAL

This situation is similar to Bid Managers' interaction with finance. The legal experts will be involved in reviewing and drawing up terms and conditions. In some cases there will be a very significant input from and interaction with, the legal department. This is particularly true of government business where the contract can be as big as the proposal itself, with literally dozens of schedules to the main contract.

The following are deliverables that typically require contributions from legal:

Deliverable	Description
Contract and schedules	Analysis of client terms and conditions comments on what is acceptable, not acceptable. Offering advice on drafting supplier terms and conditions, contracts for subcontractors and all other legally binding relationships within the sphere of the bid and ultimate supply to client.
Risk	Any risks to the bid (for example, time it will take to review the contract may be too long) or the client offering from a contractual point of view.

Key point. Changes to terms and conditions can have significant impact on the risk involved in the business. It is important to have reliable legal opinion, do not be tempted to rely on an amateur view. For example, there is a significant difference between best endeavours and reasonable endeavours. If you do not know, consult an expert, this is not a legal textbook.

BID MANAGERS AND OTHER INTERNAL DEPARTMENTS

In addition to legal and finance there will inevitably be a number of other internal departments to be satisfied with, and contribute to a bid. Most commonly they will include human resources and quality assurance,

The following are deliverables that typically require contributions from other internal resources:

Deliverable	Description
Employment policies	Training.
Health and safety	Evidence of compliance with regulations.
Personnel information	Numbers of staff employed, representation of ethnic minorities and disabled in line with, or better than, any government regulations. Contribution to local charities, investment in local community and so on.
Quality policy	Documentation and certificates relating to any formal accreditation (for example ISO9001). Copies of quality policies and procedures as required.
Quality standards	As above, documentation relating to standards. Also information on compliance with third party standards, what they mean, cost of compliance and so on.

BID MANAGERS AND SENIOR MANAGEMENT

If a bid is large enough to merit a Bid Manager, there is a very good chance that it will need support and approval from senior management. For example, where presentations have to be made at a senior level within the client organization, it shows commitment if equally senior staff are available from the would-be supplier. The other side of the coin is that there is a very good chance that the level of risk and the absolute value of the bid will be such that senior management need to be involved in approving it for submission.

The following are deliverables that typically require contributions from senior management:

Deliverable	Description
Bid approval	Provide necessary sign-off so that bid can be delivered to client.
Support	Contributing to bid in terms of being available for presentations to show commitment, writing covering letters supporting bid, promoting visibility of company at high levels.

Responsibilities of a Bid Manager

The key responsibility of the Bid Manager is to make sure that the bid gets in, complete and on time. As has been seen from the context of the role it is clear that they will need to perform a wide range of functions involving a wide range of skills. These fall naturally into a number of areas: logistical and administration; management; communication; sales and quality.

These areas may be used as a checklist (see below) – simply tick the items that apply. This will aid human resources/personnel in any required recruitment, training definitions and so forth.

Function	Roles	Required?
Logistical	Office facilities	
	Physical production	
Administration	Maintains bid file (definition of elsewhere but includes, e.g., letters, documents from client, etc.)	
	Maintain bid brief	
	Maintain other documentation as required	
	Support meetings as needed	
	Arrange distribution of documentation/information	
	Delivery of client documents	
	Risk register	
	Email and database access	
Management	Planning	
	Production of resource plan for bid	
	Risk management	
	Resource identification	
	Reporting on issues/progress	
Communication	Principal point of contact for customer (see also sales)	
	Reporting	
	Bid themes/sales themes	
	Meetings	
	Editorial	
Sales	Principal point of contact for customer	
	Input to qualification process	
	Supporting sales	
	Collates costs/budgets	
Quality	Application of organization standards	
	Manages sign-off/approvals to bid	

As mentioned earlier, there may be additional responsibilities such as owning the overall solution (if the Bid Manager has the appropriate skill set), fulfilling the project management role or having a sales function. These need to be added to the above if they apply, but they have not been included as they are additional to 'pure' bid management; not only that – the list would never end!

> *Note.* Associated with these responsibilities will be a list of deliverables that the Bid Manager is responsible for. In greater detail these will form part of the bid plan, but should be considered when defining the role. If there are no deliverables that can be defined for a role it is worth asking if the role is needed.

The reader will find more detail about what these tasks and responsibilities typically involve in the remainder of Part 1.

Example job description

What follows is a possible job description for a Bid Manager in a service or product supply industry organization. It is by no means definitive and will vary according to company needs and policy. For example, the Bid Manager may well report to finance or legal instead of to the sales organization, in which case the skill set might be quite different, perhaps with a strong emphasis on cost modelling and the prime point of contact might be sales instead of the Bid Manager. The important thing is that the job description states what the Bid Manager will do and what skills are needed to do the job. (The skills listed here are explained in greater detail in Part 3, and are included for completeness only. Similarly the functions and contents of documents/files are expanded further in Part 1; for example what should go in a bid brief and a bid file are discussed in some detail in Chapter 3.)

Job Title – Bid Manager for XY&Z Bid

Reporting to Sales Account Manager for XY&Z

Responsibilities:
Bid planning
Produce and maintain a bid brief
Identify resource requirements
Act as single point of contact for client (XY&Z)
Maintain bid file
Drive approvals process
Edit contributions to bid
Manage bid production
Collate and maintain risk registers
Manage risk process in accordance with company standards
Monitor and report bid and production costs
Produce post bid review and hand over documentation

Mandatory skills:
Project management, scheduling, planning and reporting

Risk management
Negotiation
Proposal writing

Desirable skills:
Presentations
Industry knowledge

The job description can usefully be further expanded to exclude what the Bid Manager is not to do. For example, ownership of the sales strategy might be specified as being entirely the responsibility of the sales manager and nothing to do with the Bid Manager. This is helpful in organizations where different departments have different expectations of a particular role. Of course, it is necessary to be selective when recording negative information as the list can get rather long and unhelpful. Bid Managers are not responsible for piloting the corporate jet, however much they would like to!

Summary

Having a definition of what the Bid Manager is to do is the first step towards being able to do the job effectively. A necessary second step is to have this agreed with all those with whom the Bid Manager will have to interact. These people will come from a wide range of specializations and disciplines, and will have different constraints and motivations. The Bid Manager's overall role is to get them to work together effectively.

> *Key point.* Job descriptions and terms of reference only work where all team members, and those they interact with, have matching requirements. In isolation they give responsibility without power.

Internal vs external Bid Managers

The use of freelance Bid Managers is very much an organization-dependent issue. In some companies the commercially sensitive information that a Bid Manager has access to makes the use of a freelance unacceptable. In other companies there is no problem. The author must confess to a bias at this point, for the last fifteen years all the bids I have managed have been on a freelance basis. The case for the defence is that you have no more security with a permanent person; sales staff flit from company to company all the time and have much closer contacts with the customer. Furthermore, freelance Bid Managers can bring perspectives of how other companies work, allowing a better chance of achieving best practice.

The principal downside from using freelance staff is the time it takes them to get used to the way the organization operates. A significant part of the job of a Bid Manager requires knowledge of who to talk to and who does what. For example, the Bid Manager needs to know what the approval process is for getting the bid released to the customer. For this reason many organizations that do use freelance staff tend to have a pool of Bid Managers that they call on, as they need them. This builds a long-term relationship based upon repeat business, mutual trust and familiarity with the supplier company. Another approach is to employ a freelance Bid Manager to cover a series of bids, the learning curve being overcome during the first bid. The author has positive experience of both these approaches. However, if, for example, the sales department is set against freelance staff, then it is irrelevant how good they are, they will not be able to do the job.

> *War Story.* The author has been in the situation where he was not supposed to know anything about pricing, which made managing the bid more difficult. This was largely self-defeating as in the end he did get to see 95 per cent of the pricing anyway. Given that pricing is always transitory and that a freelance would soon cease trading if found passing on significant confidences, it is hard to see why this is a problem.

Another point often made by sales staff with relation to freelance Bid Managers concerns customer perception. The Bid Manager will often act as the main point of contact for the client and sales may worry that the client may be unhappy that this person is privy to confidential information. In addition, they may perceive a lack of continuity when the freelance resource goes at the end of the bid. The counter-argument for the first point is that freelance staff are no more likely to take away confidential information than permanent staff. The second point comes under the heading of peaks and troughs; even organizations that have a steady flow of bids will have peaks and troughs that they cannot cope with internally.

Ultimately the decision on the use of freelance staff in this role is a matter for personal preference, rather than logic. If there is a strong feeling against the use of freelance staff, then the job will be impossible.

CASE STUDY

SITUATION

Karen, a freelance Bid Manager, was brought in by a multinational company to manage a bid to supply passenger display systems to an organization that owned and operated a number of international terminals. This bid involved several different operating companies within the parent organization including subsidiaries in different countries. Specifically these included display manufacture, computer supply, communications equipment, commissioning and installation. In addition input was required from quality, human resources and finance departments, and a partly owned computer software house. A further complication was that no single sales authority 'owned' the business and the responsibility for delivering a winning sales case. Although very experienced, Karen was new to this particular organization. However, her track record of managing successful bids in the same marketplace made her a sensible choice for an organization which had no permanent resource available to manage the bid.

When she asked if there were any terms of reference defining her role, and that of the people she would need to work with and get information from she was told: 'We don't really need that sort of formality here, we all know pretty much what we do already. I can tell you who to talk to if that helps at all, and I'll give you a copy of the invitation to tender (ITT) and the covering letter that went with it. Harold Bishop is the sales person for the account, he should be able to fill in some gaps.' So, Karen found herself in the situation where, other than knowing she had a bid to produce, and by when as defined in the ITT, she really did not know the boundaries of her role. Worse, she had no accurate idea what were the responsibilities of the people she would need to get information from – neither did they!

PROBLEM

So, not only did the Bid Manager not have a clearly defined role, other staff essential to the delivery of the bid did not have one either. Consequently when Karen needed to obtain critical data she had to keep going round different managers in different departments to find out who had the relevant information. This was further complicated by the inevitable different goals of each department and subsidiary organization.

For example, she needed a write-up of how the installation division would go about getting the equipment delivered and commissioned so as to provide a smooth switch over from the client's existing systems to the new equipment. All she got in reply was a standard quotation saying that, 'All out of working hours work is subject to special quotation'. The manager of the installations group was measured on installing standard displays as quickly and as cheaply as possible. Consequently, this bespoke work was not in her interest. Unfortunately, there were no terms of reference that said she had to support bids that spanned the whole of the company's operations. This meant that Karen needed to lobby for higher management support from within the part of the company she worked for and get them to negotiate with the installations management to agree to getting the non-standard work done. Not only did this take time, which was not to spare, it also meant that it took up the time of people who were also needed to provide their own input to the bid. This meant that they were late too.

This problem was repeated across the board, with the result that the whole bid got rushed out the door at the last moment without any time to review if the organization was putting forward its best case or best price. Indeed, they did not even know if it was business that they should be bidding for.

OUTCOME

The bid was lost to a competitor that had well-defined areas of responsibility that enabled their Bid Manager to gather information more easily. Consequently, there was more time to look at the overall sales position, trade off profit in one department against breakeven business in another to come up with both a better price and a more attractive overall solution. The Bid Manager cannot make the sales-winning case or the solution but can bring the information together so that those responsible can. In this case the lack of defined roles made it almost impossible for Karen to do much more than a fire-fighting exercise.

LESSON LEARNT

On arrival Karen asked her manager, the finance director of the display manufacturing subsidiary, to provide her with terms of reference for herself and also details of the roles and responsibilities of the key managers and staff she would need to martial to pull the bid together. She did not get this, but accepted the statement that they were 'not needed' at face value. As a minimum she could have written some herself and got them agreed, so covering her own position. However, she did not do this, and had both a frustrating and an unsuccessful time.

Karen strengthened her resolve to absolutely insist upon formal terms of reference defining not only what she had to do but also what contributing departments and managers had to deliver to allow her to do it. Fortunately, the company also recognized that it had a real problem and set about developing a process to support such integrated bids. Karen worked for them again on another bid with a much more satisfactory outcome.

Checklist

Item	Description	Completed?
Terms of reference and/or job description	Documentation of what the Bid Manager has the responsibility for, levels of authority, reporting requirements and so on.	
Interfaces	Definition of who the Bid Manager needs to interact with and what deliverables can be expected (in general terms).	
Deliverables	Is there a clear list of deliverable products that the Bid Manager is responsible for?	
Communication	Has this information been circulated to those who need to know?	
Conflicts	Have conflicts of interest between different departments/suppliers been defined for future resolution?	
Overlap	Where there is an overlap of responsibilities has the 'ownership' been agreed?	

3 *Methods and Approaches*

What sets us against one another is not our aims – they all come to the same thing – but our methods, which are the fruit of our varied reasoning. (St Exupery, *Wind, Sand and Stars*, 1939)

This chapter offers practical, and minimally bureaucratic, tools that you can employ to make your bid easier to deliver. They are based on the author's own experience in a number of different working environments, so doubtless owe much to a wide variety of sources. The linking factor is that they have been found to work! In addition, there is information on how formal methods can hinder the bidder and suggestions on how to minimize the impact of these.

Specific topics covered include the bid brief, internal and external reviews, benefits and disadvantages of technology, and the impact of internal and externally imposed standards (see Figure 3.1). There is a case study at the end to illustrate some of the points and a checklist for assessing the reader's own situation.

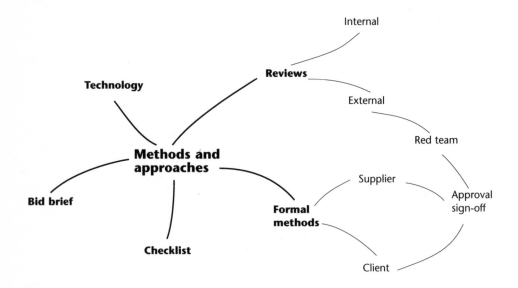

Figure 3.1 *Mind Map®: Methods and approaches*

Bid brief

This comes under the heading of, 'if you don't do anything else, at least do this'. The bid brief, bid bible, bid directive, or whatever you want to call it, is one of the most effective tools available to anyone wanting to make managing a bid less painful. In particular it will save you time.

WHAT IS IT?

The bid brief is a simple document that collates all the key information about the bid in one place. You can give it to anyone who needs to contribute to the bid, review it or approve it, and it will provide them with the essential who, why, when and what for the bid. This gives a significant benefit in terms of reducing the time it takes someone to get up to speed to work on the bid. It provides you with what amounts to an instant induction pack. Time is always at a premium when running a bid, so anything that saves time is very welcome. In addition, by having this key information documented it gives people the chance to challenge what is written there. You may think everyone knows what, for example, the win strategy for the bid is, but the effect of having it written down is amazing. Someone is bound to question it, or come up with something better. It also reduces the chances of decisions being made by default rather than consciously.

WHAT NEEDS TO BE IN IT?

The answer to this is, 'all the key information about the bid'. Typically this means some background information about the bid and the customer, key points from the sales strategy for winning the bid, elements of the plan in terms of who does what and when, and necessary administrative information. Whilst it is acceptable to refer to other documents within this bid brief, it is vital that the document works 'stand alone'. For example, you might refer to the clients request for proposal (RFP) document with regard to the timetable for the bid, but you must include any critical dates within the brief.

When considering in detail what needs to be included, the guideline is to keep it short, and to keep it simple. As a minimum the following information should be included:

INTRODUCTION	What the bid brief is for, intended audience, confidentiality, who the bid is to and any change control and distribution information.
The bid environment	This section provides a synopsis of why the procurement is happening and why you are bidding for it.
The customer's business	What the client/prospect does and how this procurement fits in with this business.
Supplier and the client position	Your relationship to the client, standing with the client, strengths and weaknesses with relation to this procurement.
Procurement scope	The size and value of the procurement, what is to be supplied to meet the needs of the customer, how long the contract will run for and related items.
Significant dates in the procurement process	When key events, such as issue of a requirements document, date for submission of a tender and so forth occur.
Contacts	Names, phone numbers, emails, job titles for key customer staff, may include rules as to who may/may not contact them directly. Any customer restrictions on contact.

Approach	A summary of how you are going to go about winning this business.
Win strategy	The overall sales strategy for winning the business, what will be the driving forces behind the sales campaign; consequently, what are the key points that any deliverable documents, presentations and so on need to make.
Evaluation criteria	Where known, the criteria that the client intends to use for evaluating the bid. In the case of many government procurements these are issued with the requirements/tender documentation. In other cases it is a sales function and intelligence-gathering exercise to identify these. Even when they are stated there may be hidden agendas. If you do not have a clear idea about these, you should ask yourself why you are bidding!
Competitors	Who are the competitors, brief assessment of their strengths and weaknesses (refer to separate SWOT-type analyses if required, but include key points here). Any potential for partner companies should be identified here. (Chapter 13, Sales, describes the SWOT process in some detail.)
Proposal themes	Key themes that need to be incorporated in the bid, at all levels, to support the sales case. The goal is to make all deliverables support the same, persuasive, story.
Proposal plan	Basic plan giving key events and when they need to happen, together with information on who does what.
The bid team organization	A chart supporting the who does what elements of the plan.
Bid production milestone plan	A table giving all the identified milestones for the plan and the deliverables required for their completion.
Sign-off	Who signs off the bid, what are the criteria, what is the process?
Constraints	Any restrictions imposed by the supplier organization or the client organization in terms of compliance with quality assurance rules. For example, there may be specific reports that need to be made, formats to be followed, procedures to be completed. These should be noted to ensure that everyone working on the bid knows they apply. This is particularly important if temporary, third party and freelance staff are involved who are unlikely to know about the reports etc.

In addition you might include some of the following (but only if it helps):

Development methodology	A description of how the bid will be developed in terms of the reviews, quality control, document control and issue.
The bid structure	The contents of any document for delivery to the client, e.g. a proposal.
Responsibility matrix	A detailed breakdown of who is responsible for delivering what, to the level of individual answers, sections and so on in any proposal document. This should cover all items included in the bid structure, plus any additional deliverables such as customer presentations.
Proposal development standards	Text and artwork standards, terminology and grammar details of document templates, fonts, layout and so on.

MAINTENANCE

Yes, the bid brief does need to be maintained. It is one of the jobs the Bid Manager needs to do. Indeed, it should be part of the bid file (see Chapter 5 on administration and logistics) and so forms part of the core documentation for the bid.

Reviews

One of the more important things to do with any bid is get it reviewed. This applies just as much to the sales and business case as it does to the solution offered and the proposal itself. Reviews should take place at every key stage in the bidding process and should include (frequently) internal reviews, and (less frequently, key stage) external reviews.

INTERNAL REVIEWS

These include reviews of the proposed solution/proposition, peer reviews, proofreading and formatting done by the bid team itself. The frequency and timing of these will vary from bid to bid and will be driven by the needs of the bid team. Such reviews are part of the process of refining the bid. For parts of the bid where only one team member understands the technicalities, these reviews will be limited to checking on the clarity of what is written/said against the overall strategy for winning the bid.

Where documents are to be reviewed outside the bid team, there should be as full as possible review by the team itself before this happens. The Bid Manager will need to plan and organize the internal reviews in conjunction with the team.

It is an administrative role of the Bid Manager to make sure that these reviews take place and have the support needed to be successful (see Chapter 5).

EXTERNAL REVIEWS, WHY HAVE THEM?

The point of these reviews is to make sure that the content is correct and that there is a viable solution and business case behind the bid. They should not be confused with proofreading, though the overall goal of achieving a better end product is similar. They act as quality control on the bidding process. It is important to note that such reviews are not an overhead on the project, and should not be seen as such; they are an active part of developing the bid and the cost is part of the cost of sale.

There are five principal benefits that come from having such reviews:

1   You get the benefit of independent opinion on the team's ideas.
2   The review team will usually come up with new ideas of their own.
3   Endorsement by third party helps with the approval process.
4   The quality assurance role helps eliminate major misconceptions and mistakes.
5   An opinion of what a customer might think is obtained as a sanity check.

EXTERNAL REVIEW PROCESS

The process is very simple and is presented here so that the Bid Manager will know to allow sufficient time for it to take place. It comprises:

1 Identify point(s) where review(s) is/are due, for example four weeks before document delivery to client.
2 Decide on review team members, get their commitment (and their managers' if needed).
3 Book meeting rooms as needed.
4 Produce reviewers' briefing document – issue it to reviewers.
5 Two/three days before review is required issue draft bid documents to review team. Try not to make it less than two days if possible.
6 The review team presents the findings, together with marked up drafts/edited electronic copies and so on to the bid team in a meeting moderated by the Bid Manager.
7 The bid team assesses the feedback and decides upon response, keeping the reviewers up to date for the next stage.

> *Note.* There is a natural hiatus once the documents have gone for review, the team should use this time to prepare for what comes next, to chase up loose ends, etc. The team should not be allowed to lose momentum during the short time the bid is being reviewed.

RED TEAMS AND BLACK TEAMS

Bid Managers often bandy about these jargon words. They have a very simple translation: the 'Black' team writes the bid, the 'Red' team reviews it. Within this book the team writing the bid, often called the Black team, will be referred to as the bid team, and the reviewing team will be known as the Red team. This is a purely arbitrary decision of the author, you may call these teams anything you like. Indeed, Red teams are regularly called anything you like, and more!

> *Key point.* The Red team will help prevent the bid team from suffering from group think (see Chapter 11, Teams). They will get an outside view that will test the validity of the proposition.

An additional benefit relates to any qualification/approval processes that may exist within the organization. The Red team review points provide an independent view on the value of proceeding with the bid and, providing any negative points are addressed, this will go a long way towards building a case to proceed.

COMPOSITION OF RED TEAMS

A Red team needs to comprise people not involved in producing the bid (that is, independent). They then review the proposition at various stages from the point of view of the customer and the company. Typically, this means that you need a team that includes people with the relevant technical knowledge, industry knowledge, an understanding of the financial issues, contractual knowledge and sales expertise. Ideally a Red team should not have more than five members to avoid the committee effect. This effect comes about where everyone needs to make points on every topic and consensus needs to be reached by the whole group on every point made. Red teams need to be 'lean and mean' as they do not have the luxury of the extended timetable required for long-winded discussion.

For example, take the case of a water company bidding to provide all the water supply and wastewater disposal and processing for a large industrial site. The Red team would need to have specialists capable of reviewing the compliance with statutory regulations, the engineering solution, the pricing and the legal liabilities, together with someone who understood what makes a good sales case to an industrial user.

For small bids, and those where there is not a complex solution, it may be possible to combine some of the roles within one individual. For example, in the case of supplying a large number of desktop computers against a client-supplied specification it might be possible to combine the legal, pricing and sales case into one role with a second person making sure that the technical specifications were met. When putting together review teams, available resource will be limited and the Bid Manager will need to take a pragmatic approach.

Note. In some organizations with established bid teams it is possible for one team to act as the Red team for another bid team. This reduces briefing time.

BRIEFING RED TEAMS

One of the jobs of the Bid Manager is to brief the Red team (or any other reviewer) on what it is being asked to do. As a minimum the team will need all the information that is in the bid directive/brief. It needs to know the background to the bid, why the bid is being made, information about the client and the competition, the timetable and so forth. The team also needs to know what it is reviewing for. In addition, it needs to know logistical items such as when and where the team is to meet, and when and where it is to give its feedback to the bid team.

Where the reviewing team is made up of a mixture of specialist and management staff, it is essential that each of these is given an individual area, relevant to their role/expertise to concentrate on.

Hint. Ask the team to concentrate on content rather than format – it will tell you what the team thinks of the presentation anyway (people cannot help it!) but this will steer the team away from spending all its time on typographical errors.

RED TEAM BRIEF STRUCTURE

1 Introduction	What the document is for, what we are bidding for. (High level only. Do not repeat detailed information that is in the bid brief/directive).
2 Situation	Overview of situation, as seen by Bid Manager/team, objectives.
3 Responsibilities	Which member of the Red team should review which part of the bid.
4 Timetable	When documents will be issued etc.
5 Meetings	Where the team can meet, where debrief can take place.

EXAMPLE BRIEF

Introduction

This is the Red team briefing document for the proposal to NB plc for the supply of facilities management services. It should be read in conjunction with the bid brief that was issued on 17 November.

Situation

BS plc is submitting its proposal as a long listed supplier (one of 12) with the intention of becoming one of three short-listed suppliers, possibly in partnership with one or more of the other bidders on the long list. The bid needs to be submitted on 2 December by 15.00 hours. At this stage we are not sure if we will need a partner company (or more) so the bid should be viewed as a stand-alone one. The Red team's primary objective is to review the bid on this basis, but point out where it thinks a partnership approach would be beneficial.

Responsibilities

Mike D. to review sales case and terms and conditions. Jackie F. to review technical solution. Helen A. to review service offering, and service levels. James C. to perform sanity checks on costs and estimated revenue. All to review from customer perspective. *Note*: the document will have many spelling and typing errors, general formatting problems and so on. Please feel free to mark these up on your paper copies, but note that these are not part of your brief. Any comments on presentation are welcomed.

Timetable

The proposal draft will be issued to all Red team members on 21 November at 12.30 hours both on paper and electronically. The debrief meeting has been scheduled for 12.30 on 23. There will be a follow-up presentation to the Red team on 28 November, time permitting, to inform the Red team of the bid team's resolution of any issued raised at the debrief meeting. If time is short, the Red team will either be emailed or briefed individually.

   Note: Red team members were issued with the client requirement documents, draft terms and conditions and risk register with the bid brief on 17 November.

Meetings

The Lassiter room has been booked all day on 22 November for use of the Red team and from 14.00 to 16.00 on 23 November for the debrief meeting

PROCESSING RED TEAM FEEDBACK

There is a significant danger with Red team feedback. The comments from the reviewing team can easily be taken negatively and lead to a decline in bid team moral. Consequently, it is absolutely vital that the Bid Manager makes sure that both the bid team and the Red team understand that no personal criticisms are intended. Making the spokesperson for the Red team someone who is experienced in the process and will present the point in a positive way can help with this.

   For example, rather than say, 'this will never work, you've forgotten all about the fact that the client has five factories in different parts of the country!' you can ask, 'how will the solution be expanded to cope with locations in different parts of the country?' That said, there will be limited time available for this work and some comments, particularly on marked-up drafts, will be terse. The Bid Manager needs to reinforce the need not to take things personally and see the Red team comments as 'free' consultancy. This is effectively what it is, as far as the bid team is concerned.

> *Key point*. It should be noted that the feedback from the Red team represents its opinion, and the bid team does not have to follow it. However, all points made should be considered and accepted or discarded for a reason.

War story. The author worked on one bid where the Red team identified a significant number of shortcomings in the draft where the question asked by the client in their request for information (RFI) had not been answered. The bid team had simply copied over answers to *similar* questions from earlier proposals. Although similar these were not actually the same and the client would have scored the responses very poorly. After all, it is really very rude to ignore the question asked and answer one that suits you, as is demonstrated by politicians every day. The Red team correctly identified that the bid read in a very slapdash and arrogant way and this is how the client would see it. However, even more useful was a suggestion from one of the Red team that the client was known to have a short-term space problem pending relocation to new premises. This was not stated in the RFI, though the relocation was. So, any proposition that would help them solve this short-term problem would be of significant benefit. Offering to site technical support staff on the supplier's premises instead of the client's, prior to the move, made the proposition attractive to the client and was mentioned in the debrief prior to moving on to the next, shortlist, stage of the procurement.

Information technology

There is a wide range of information technology (IT) tools that can be used to support the production and management of a bid. Because these change rapidly no attempt will be made to give a definitive list, or to suggest which ones are best. Instead, facilities and applications that may be available to the Bid Manager are listed together with what they may be useful for. It is left as an exercise for the reader to determine which, if any, of these are available within the Bid Manager's organization. References to individual products do not indicate an endorsement, simply that the author has come across them.

Facility	Advantages	Disadvantages
Email	Makes it easy to pass notes and information between people on the bid quickly and with little or no geographic limitations. Can also be used to circulate draft documents for review.	One danger with email is that people stop talking to each other. Rather than sort a problem out with a single conversation by the coffee machine a series of often escalatingly irritated exchanges can take place without any resolution of the real problem.
Database	A database can be an effective way of both sharing information and distributing documents such as a bid directive, meeting notes, drafts for review and so on.	Resource is required to administer the database; temporary, third party and freelance staff may need training to be able to use it – this may take up too much time in some cases. If this is the only repository for vital information, it needs to be very reliable.
Intranet	Many organizations have an intranet – a web site accessible only to its own employees and other authorized users. It may be possible to use this as a source of company information and as a place for posting information to be looked at by the bid team, irrespective of location.	It may not be as secure as you think. You should also question how up to date the company information is. For example, it is not unknown for a product that has been withdrawn from sale still to be on the company intranet. This may be deliberate for support reasons or simply because nobody has updated it yet.

Internet	The Internet can be a very useful source of information. As a minimum you should investigate any web sites your client may have. Many government standards and briefing papers are available here.	Be aware that if you can access it, so can anyone else. So confidential information should not be placed there and you should assume that your competitors have access to anything you do.
Word processing (WP)	Taken as read, but it is essential that there is someone within the bid team who is expert with whatever package is in use. It is reasonable to expect all bid team members to be able to create basic text files even if they cannot use all of the features.	Needs to be controlled if the individual sections of the document are not going to get distinctly inconsistent in appearance and style. If you can, get an editor or WP specialist who can manage this.
Desktop publishing (DTP)	Can help produce a superior end product, though most WP systems are satisfactory for the majority bids and proposals.	Unlike WP it is unlikely that all members of the bid team will be familiar with the DTP system. The team will be dependent on staff who can use it. Its use should be restricted to specialist areas, for example the design of a special cover for a proposal document.
Printing/ reproduction	The more of this that is under the team's direct control, the better off you will be. Having printers, copiers and binding and production equipment makes the bid team that much less subject to non-availability of such equipment at what is always a critical time.	There is an administrative burden associated with keeping stocks of paper, toner and ink cartridges, binding materials and any other essential supplies. These also take up space. Given a choice the author would always take on this burden rather than rely on a corporate infrastructure whose priorities are not in line with those of a bid team. Consider having at least a fallback position of one printer that is under team control.
Presentation equipment	As with the production equipment having a dedicated projector, flip chart and other related items makes the bid team self-reliant.	As for production equipment. Arguably worth the overhead if you can get it.

Formal methods and standards

Within the bid brief there was a section relating to formal standards. These can lead to certain constraints being placed upon the bid team. For example, there may be restrictions as to where you place your organization's logo on any delivered documentation. Similarly, the client may have a specific project management methodology that you have to follow for the project related areas of your proposal. It is important that these are adhered to. Failing to follow internal rules may delay approval of your bid for submission to the client; worse you may find yourself having to revisit work already done. You do not have time for this, so get it right from the beginning. Following client standards is even more important as you will only find out after you have put forward your bid, when it is too late and all your efforts will have been wasted.

Consequently, it is essential that the Bid Manager or someone appointed to do so, checks on both internal and external standards that may apply. Note that such standards include environmental, health and safety, procurement practices, personnel and human resources, technical standards, quality assurance and a wide range of other possibilities. In some cases this is a major exercise in its own right and needs to be identified sooner rather than later in the bid process.

Finally, the Bid Manager must become familiar with any sign-off and approval processes that must be completed before any bid is released to a client.

CASE STUDY

SITUATION

Libby K was an experienced Bid Manager who had worked for the parent company for several years. She had worked as both a Bid Manager and a project manager on the delivery side so had a good understanding of the problems that would spring up. She was given charge of the bid to NB plc because of this experience and because the bid involved working with a wide variety of contributors to the bid. This was seen as a key opportunity for the company and considered to be a 'must win' opportunity.

PROBLEM AND APPROACH

The key issue for this particular bid was the need to use a wide range of specialist staff to produce relatively small, but vital, sections of the bid. Many of these staff were on assignment to fee-paying clients, others worked for partner companies over which Libby had no direct control. Consequently, they would have to 'hit the floor running' and produce their contribution in a short time. Unfortunately they would need to understand both the context of their work and how it fitted in with the overall sales pitch.

Libby's approach was to adopt the concept of a bid brief, something she had seen in the past, though not used regularly by her employer. This was a short document of about 10 pages that encapsulated the essence of the bid.

OUTCOME

The bid was produced without too much grief. Libby's experience saw to it that there was sufficient resource to produce the required hard and soft copy documentation. On its own this was a major contribution to the bid team having the time to focus on getting the sales case across to the prospective client. However, without the specialist input the bid would have failed. The use of the bid brief provided effective briefing for the specialists so they could work when available and still fit in with the overall sales strategy.

LESSON LEARNT

By producing the bid brief (or bid bible/bid directive as it is sometimes called) Libby had a single, very manageable document that she was able to use to brief the people who needed to work on the bid. Because the document was short it was easy for her to maintain and re-circulate it to keep staff up to date. So, everyone involved in writing and reviewing the bid was always contributing in concert with the rest of the team, even when they were working remotely.

Checklist

Item	Description	Completed?
Bid brief	Do you have a document that includes: (a) The customer's business (b) Supplier and client current position (c) Procurement scope (d) Significant dates (e) Contacts (f) Win strategy (g) Evaluation criteria (h) Competitors (i) Proposal themes (j) Bid team (k) Bid production milestones (l) Sign-off and constraints on bid (m) Anything else (if) useful?	
Internal reviews	What reviews are required? Is there a defined timetable for this? Are there meeting rooms available, etc.?	
External reviews	Have you produced a brief for the reviewers? Do they know when they need to do the review? Have they agreed to it? Have they been circulated the information they need? Have they been provided with meeting space? Has a meeting been booked for feedback?	
Supporting technology	Email: does everyone have access? Database: is there someone to administer it? Does everyone have access? Intranet: Does everyone have access? Is it secure? Internet Word processing DTP Printing/reproduction Presentation equipment	
Formal methods and standards	Has someone been appointed to check on these? Have the approval and sign-off requirements been identified?	
Company methodology	Is there a company methodology that needs to be followed? Have you used it? Do you need to do more in order to provide a bid brief/directive?	
Client methodology	Does the customer require you to use any specific tools/processes in order to bid? Have you followed them?	

4 Risk Management

Everything is sweetened by risk. (Alexander Smith, 1863)

Risk management is a mature process, which grew out of painful lessons learnt in high-risk industries such as military, nuclear and drug manufacture where real life/death issues had to be considered. Major disasters such as the nuclear incident at Three Mile Island provided an impetus to risk management, and it is commonplace in these arenas and has proved itself to be effective. It has also moved out into national and local government. For example, assessment of risk from flooding is now a significant part of planning approval for housing provision. Developers are required to look at historic data to see how often the land has been flooded. The authorities will specify an acceptable level of risk, for example once in 50 years, that must be demonstrated before the developer can go ahead and build. This is the essence of risk management: how likely is something to happen and what will be its impact?

In the commercial arena events such as the Ford Pinto scandal stands out as a case where risk management could have saved the day. Ford management judged that the damages claims that they would sustain from the number of people killed or injured by the explosion of a badly sited petrol tank were less than the cost of re-engineering the car to put the tank in a safer place. When they were found out they were justly punished for a cynical act. However, even with the low moral standards of the people involved, proper risk management might have identified that there was a potentially high-impact risk of punitive

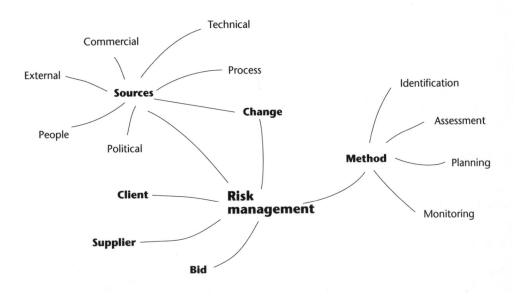

Figure 4.1 *Mind Map®: Risk*

damages. The organization could have been protected from the actions of a corrupt minority.

Consequently, risk management is now common in most government and commercial organizations and is seen as an accepted and valuable process. However, with the focus firmly on the risks from implementation, the risks involved in bidding are often overlooked. The emphasis tends to be on the risks involved in delivering the products and services to the client and potential impact on the supplier organization. This chapter provides an overview of risk, risk analysis and management to the depth required by a Bid Manager (see Figure 4.1). It is not intended to be a complete training course in risk management, those requiring this are referred to the Additional Reading at the end of this book. However, there is sufficient information here to enable a Bid Manager to run an effective risk management programme for a bid. The emphasis on risks and the examples given here will be mainly related to bids.

> *Note.* Although the focus here is on risks to the bid, there will always be an overlap between these and risks to delivery.

Risk management – a potted guide

Figure 4.2 shows a standard approach that is common to many risk management approaches, including those used in formal methodologies such as PRINCE 2 (see Glossary). It involves a repeating cycle of identification, assessment, planning and monitoring throughout the life of a project. This works for any industry or market sector, being a simple and well-proven cycle.

Figure 4.2   *Standard approach to risk management*

SOURCES OF RISK

There are six categories that are normally used to identify the sources of risk to a bid or project. They include: external; political; commercial technical; people and processes. The following list shows instances of these sources of risk:

External	These can be anything from acts of terrorism and earthquakes at one end of the scale to a traffic jam making the timely delivery of a key document impossible at the other.
Political	Change of government, political issues within an organization. For example, if you are bidding for a Public Private Partnership and a general election is looming there might be a risk of the bid being either cancelled or delayed as a result.
Commercial	An example of commercial risk would be where the client company was financially unsound. There would be a risk of not getting paid for services and/or goods delivered if the client were to cease trading. Takeover bids are another source of commercial risk. There is also a risk that, if the estimates are poor or based upon incomplete information, the business won may be unprofitable.
Technical	Technology does not meet the performance predicted by the designers. In a bid there may be a requirement to run some observed performance tests to demonstrate that the proposed solution was tenable. If the technology was in any way unknown, there would be a risk associated with such a test.
People	Key staff members leave or are sick at a critical point. Staff do not have the skills required to do the job in hand.
Processes	Company procedures might have so great a bureaucratic overhead that it might be too onerous to produce a bid within acceptable timescales. It might be too difficult to obtain approval to do something that a customer requires that is out of the ordinary.

In some cases it is fairly arbitrary which category a risk comes into, for example a change of government is both political and probably external to the project. The important thing is that you check that you have looked at all these potential sources of risk when identifying them.

CHANGE

In addition to these risks there is also the major, overall source of risk: CHANGE! In fact all the risks categorized above only become real if something changes. For example, take the risk of a supplier becoming insolvent. It only becomes real when the change happens. If everything stayed the same there would be no risks in the first place. The corollary of this is that change is of itself a source of risk. Whenever there is a change risk needs to be revisited. Change can simply mean the passage of time, as well as a change in requirements or circumstance. So, risks need to be monitored as the bid progresses. Risk identification, and the risk management process as whole, needs to be constantly revisited throughout the life of a bid or project.

RISK IDENTIFICATION

Identifying risk is essentially a matter of asking those involved in the bid where they see risks to the bid/delivered solution coming from. The Bid Manager will need to manage this process and ensure that all the raw information is captured. The baseline information needed includes a description of the source of the risk, an estimate of the impact and the probability of the risk happening. A sample form that could be used for capturing this information is shown in Figure 4.3. However, an entry in a notebook will suffice!

Risk #	Severity *High* High/Medium/Low	Probability *Low* High/Medium/Low	Date *12/January '02*
Description			
Cancellation due to change of education policy			
Interviewer: *David Nickson*		Interviewee: *Suzy Siddons*	

Figure 4.3   *Risk identification notebook entry*

The following list makes suggestions as to whom you should involve in the identification of risks:

Internal staff
:   These include all the members of the bid team, anyone who has done similar work before for the same or a similar client, staff who would be involved in implementing what is sold to the client and any experts with relevant specialist knowledge that are not covered by the above.

External staff
:   Similar staff from partner companies.
    Client staff, if available, to get their views, though this is more relevant to the risks to the delivery rather than risks to the bid itself.

Finally, there are essentially three ways of going about the risk identification that the author has seen tried. They all have their pros and cons and are summarized below:

Memo/email
:   *Method* – sending out an all points bulletin to the staff identified asking them to write down what they think and return it to you for collation into an initial risk register. Any relevant briefing material should be included with the email/memo and a reasonable deadline should be set.
    Pros – staff have time to think about their response before replying. A geographically disparate audience or one where scheduling is very difficult can be accommodated.
    Cons – staff make their risk identifications in isolation so there is both repetition which wastes time and no cross-fertilization of ideas, which means that some risks may well be missed.

Brainstorming meeting
:   *Method* – a meeting is set up with all, or as many as possible, of the risk identifiers present. Everyone is provided with the briefing documents a reasonable time in advance of this meeting. The risk sources are then brainstormed in turn with a moderator note taker as required. The results are converted into a risk register and assessed and so forth after the meeting.
    Pros – this is usually very efficient in terms of time; a risk only has to be identified once, and is beneficial in that people 'spark off each other' and

produce risks that would not occur to them in isolation.

Cons – if the meeting is not run effectively then all that will happen is that huge amounts of time will be wasted in trying to solve problems, argue as to whether or not a risk is worth considering, what would be a better way of doing it and so on. In other words, to be creative the brainstormers need to be controlled.

Individual interviews
Method – each contributor is interviewed and asked to say what the risks are within each category. Any relevant briefing material should be sent before the meeting and some thinking time should be scheduled before the interview is to take place. It may be necessary to give an introduction to those who have not taken part in a similar exercise before so they know what is required, what a risk is and so on. The results are compiled as per the email/memo approach. These interviews can be made using phone or video links if person to person meeting is not practical.

Pros – the time between scheduling the interview and conducting it gives people time to think in advance of the meeting. The interviewer also has the chance to clarify understanding and prompt with information about other risks that have been identified. This method has been shown to work well.

Cons – this can take a long time if it requires many interviews spread over a number of separate locations. It also does not have the benefit that comes from individual suggestions sparking off new ideas in other people that you get from the brainstorming approach.

Ideally the best way is to use the brainstorming method, followed up by an email/memo with the findings attached, to give people a 'second bite at the cherry'. But, as is often the case, logistical restrictions will usually force some combination of all the methods. Pragmatism is the Bid Manager's watchword.

RISK REGISTER

Once risks have been identified they need to be recorded so that they can be assessed, and contingency plans made and updated throughout the life of the project. Many organizations' formal methodologies have their own way of recording risks. The example shown here is typical of most and will serve as a stand-in for where no standard exists:

- *Risk identity (ID)*: each risk is given a unique ID for future reference, where a risk is removed from the register, its number is not reused in case it is necessary to refer back to it at a future time. It is recommended to remove risks once they have been closed or eliminated so that the risk register shows only those that are currently active. In many bids this will not be necessary because of the duration of the bid and the risks involved are sufficiently few for it not to matter.
- *Description*: a brief description of the source of the risk and why it will impact the bid.
- *Impact*: severity of impact, for example Low (L), Medium (M) and High (H). High would cover a risk that would prevent the bid from being delivered, or from being successful.
- Probability: chances of the bid being affected by the risk. Again, the suggestion is for a simple Low (L), Medium (M) and High (H) assessment. You should be able to ignore any low probability events.
- *Contingency plan/owner*: what is planned to be done to minimize the risk (either by reducing the chances of it happening or by reducing the impact of the event). It is important that there is an owner for this plan who is responsible both for putting it in

place and reporting on how the risk changes with time. During the risk identification phase this entry may be blank.

- *Date*: this is the date that the risk was last assessed. It may be desirable to add closed (C) or Open (O) to this date to indicate if the risk is still relevant (see comment in 'Risk identity' above).

For example:

Risk ID	Description	Impact	Prob.	Contingency plan/owner	Date
1	Minor changes to customer requirements	L	H		12/6/04
2	Competition for technical resource required to design solution.	H	M		12/6/04

> *Note.* Where a bid or project has several distinct elements, for example, equipment supply and support services it may be helpful to expand the Risk ID to show this. E1...n for Equipment, S1...n for Services.

RISK ASSESSMENT

Once risks have been identified then they need to be assessed. Again, various methods have been used but they generally consist of a combination probability of the event happening and the impact it will have if it does. These were captured during the risk identification exercise earlier. In organizations employing formal methods, such as PRINCE, there may a specified process for assessing and reviewing risks. If so, the Bid Manager needs to both follow the approved processes and allow time for doing so. If not, the Bid Manager, in conjunction with those who 'own' the business risks, sales prospect, and so on should make the assessment.

The following offers a simple set of criteria that could be used for this purpose:

Impact/probability	Ranking
High impact high probability	Very high – unacceptable
High impact medium probability	High – potentially unacceptable
Medium impact high probability	High
Medium impact medium probability	Medium
All other combinations	Low

Typically all those ranked below medium can safely be ignored for the purpose of the bid. You may choose to monitor those ranked as medium. However, they should be kept as a matter of record, and can be revisited if matters change sufficiently to make them a threat. The resulting risk register should be circulated to all those working directly on the bid.

> *Issue*: Visibility of risks. A risk register is often a deliverable to the client. There may be occasions when this needs some careful handling. For example, there might be a risk to your bid that one of your competitors has a better technology than is available to yourself. This would be a risk to your bid, but not to the customer project. It would seem reasonable, and well advised, to exclude this risk from the register you deliver to the client. This may seem an obvious example, but it can become less clear cut after the event. You might win the business

and then have a problem delivering the solution because of this. You would then need to defend your position to the client as to why this was not identified earlier. It is important to make sure that any risks you hide from the client really are risks that only apply to your bid. The cases where the bid was threatened because of insufficient internal resource is clearly a private matter.

RISK PLANNING

Once risks have been assessed, the next stage is to establish who will have responsibility for each risk and produce a plan for containing the risk.

A risk plan need not be complex, indeed it is typically just an action that needs to be taken to minimize the probability of a risk happening or to mitigate its impact. Some risks can neither be mitigated nor reduced in probability; in these cases the risk has to be accepted if the project is to continue. However, this should be a conscious decision.

Key point. Risk should be taken knowingly, not by default. Risks that you do not know about are of unlimited impact and probability. It is not possible to know every single risk, but the more you identify the better the chances of a realistic price.

At this stage a risk register for a bid will look something like this:

Risk ID	Description	Impact	Prob.	Contingency plan/owner	Date
1	Minor changes to customer requirements	L	H	Bid Manager to monitor changes as they come in from client and circulate for impact assessment.	14/6/04
2	Competition for technical resource required to design solution.	H	M	Sales manager to make case to main board and Bid Manager to look at use of freelance staff.	14/6/04

RISK MONITORING

The risk process cannot be considered as a one-off. The risks need to be revisited on a regular basis; for a bid this should be at least weekly. This monitoring should include asking if any new risks have been identified, which then need to be recorded, assessed and planned for in the usual way. As a matter of course the risk register should be revisited every time a major change occurs, for example a change in timetable, major change in customer requirements or an approach to a partner with another bidder.

The Bid Manager must make sure both that the risks relating to the project, often a client deliverable, are kept up to date and that the risks that apply to the bid itself are maintained. The bid-specific risks are likely to be very confidential and would be of considerable interest to any competitor and might also undermine the confidence of the customer in the bidder. For this reason they should have a controlled circulation.

Sample risk for bids

As described earlier the sources of risk are external, political, commercial, technical, people and processes. The list below gives some example risks for a bid within these categories. This example is loosely based upon an outsourcing procurement for an EMEA (Europe and Middle East Area) wide manufacturing company. The bid involved a number of specialist suppliers in addition to the prime contractor company that provided the Bid Manager.

External	(a)	Competitors have more influence over the client. An incumbent supplier may well have better access to the decision makers than a competitor, thus influencing requirements in their favour.
	(b)	Physical disasters may impact ability to deliver the bid (fire, flood, and terrorist action).
	(c)	Subcontractors not willing to trade with supplier or in difficulty and so on.
Political	(a)	Government policy change on company cars affecting viability of a fleet operation contract – impact on residual values of cars due to increased taxation.
	(b)	Changes in trade laws may affect ability to supply services and equipment across national boundaries.
	(c)	Government procurements can be affected, delayed or even cancelled when government changes complexion.
	(d)	Key client staff are known to be biased against supplier.
Commercial	(a)	The financial viability of one of the subcontractors could affect the ability to deliver all the equipment within the required timescale.
	(b)	The business may not be profitable when won.
	(c)	Exchange rates may impact profitability or chances of winning in multinational deals.
	(d)	Terms and conditions contain penalties, risks and so forth that are not acceptable to supplier.
Technical	(a)	Technical information supplied by client may be insufficient to produce risk free solution.
	(b)	Need to involve third party to supply key components for solution.
	(c)	Technical solution unproven, leading-edge technology involved, reliance on third parties not changing de facto standards.
People	(a)	Sales staff may be poached by a rival company.
	(b)	Lack of resource to complete the bid.
	(c)	Staff dislike for client based on previous experience; hard to build good working relationship.
Processes	(a)	Company processes can take too long to fit in with rate of change inherent in bids.
	(b)	Client processes, for example compliance with a particular documentation and management standard, can make delivering supporting information for the bid too onerous.

Key point. A major risk to any bid is lack of information. This is irrespective of which category is being considered. The bottom line is that if you cannot get the best price the assumptions that you make will either add up to an unacceptable price, or put you in a position of unbounded and therefore unacceptable risk.

Example bid risk plan

The risks given below, complete with their impact and a short contingency plan, are typical of those that might be found in a large commercial, multinational bid. No Low/Low risks have been included, and anything less than MM (or HL) has been listed.

Risk ID	Description	Impact	Prob.	Contingency plan/owner	Date
	External				
1	Legislation may change affecting working hours in the UK. Would not affect European elements of bid.	M	M	No action, monitor risk.	12/6/06
2	Changes to scope of procurement. Would affect all bidders equally.	M	M	No action, monitor risk.	12/6/06
3	One of the main competitors is sitting tenant and may have undue influence on procurement. This may give them an advantage.	H	M	Sales manager to establish if this is the case and, if so, either ask for 'level playing field' or review validity of bidding.	12/6/06
	Political				
5	Potential trade escalation in trading restrictions between USA and Europe may impact cost and delivery of computer equipment.	M	M	Monitor risk – sales manager	12/6/06
	Commercial				
6	Exchange rate fluctuations may impact revenue.	M	H	Finance manager to consider currency options trades to manage this to acceptable levels.	12/6/06
7	Business may not be sufficiently profitable within the client's budget.	H	M	Sales manager to establish the budget as soon as possible if too low, then re-evaluate bid/ no bid decision and/or negotiate scope of supply with client.	12/6/06
	Technical				
8	Network performance across country boundaries may be too low on existing client equipment.	M	H	Technical manager to establish additional cost of upgrading the existing network as a contingency charge.	12/6/06
	People				
	Availability of temporary administrative staff to produce bid documents for distribution.	H	L	Monitor risk – consider a print bureau as back-up solution – Bid Manager.	12/6/06
	Process				
9	The approval process for high-value projects requires international board-level staff including the senior finance and sales vice presidents and the chief executive officer. If this cannot be organized in time then the bid cannot be presented.	H	M	Bid Manager to schedule meetings in the week prior to bid delivery. If complete approval cannot be completed, then key points to be agreed for individual approval by delivery date.	12/6/06

> *Note*: the missing Risk ID's number (4) belongs to those risks that have been eliminated prior to this stage.

Risk as a deliverable

Although this chapter has concentrated on risk as it relates to the bid it is also very likely that there will be two other parties interested in risk – the client and the supplier.

RISK FOR THE CLIENT

It is quite common for the client to ask what risks the supplier sees in delivering the solution, product or services to the client. This needs to be carefully considered. It is important to be open and honest about the risks that you see but it is important to make sure that you put as positive a case as possible. Showing that the risks are both understood and that positive plans exist to control them will make a client more comfortable with the proposal. However, where risks apply more to your organization than the competitor's a cautious approach needs to be taken. The sales elements of this are discussed in Chapter 13, but the Bid Manager should expect a sales and marketing input to the risk register and plan.

When putting together the risk documentation for the client, use the client format if specified. If none is specified then make sure that your presentation is clear, unambiguous and attractively presented. The examples that are provided within this chapter should be acceptable.

RISK FOR THE SUPPLIER

It is suggested that the bid and supplier risk registers be maintained within a single risk register. However, it should be split into two separate sections, one relating solely to the bid, the other relating to the supply to the client. These risks will cover all aspects of fulfilling the client requirement including technical, commercial, market presence and relationship with the client. They may include risks that are commercially sensitive.

These risks will come from the same sources as identified before but will emphasize the risks that come from delivering the business. Inevitably there will be some overlap here and Bid Managers need to use their own judgement. It is more important that the risks be captured, assessed and planned for than that they end up in the correct part of the risk ID list.

This combined risk document will be significant when making any bid/no bid decisions. If it is not then the Bid Manager should suggest that it becomes so!

CASE STUDY

SITUATION

A major IT outsourcing company had the opportunity to bid for the complete IT infrastructure including the desktop (personal computers [PCs] and application software), the networks and servers, the day-to-day operation (help desk, training and so on) for a large financial institution. This represented the chance to gain additional revenue in excess of £10 million per year. The prospect was a very good one as it required the supply of the 'bread and butter' services that the company understood very well.

Brian A, senior project manager, was given the dual role of managing a bid and contributing the project management part of the overall solution. Brian had considerable experience in the delivery of such services. Indeed, he had set up similar operations for his employer in the past. He also had some experience in working on bids, though more as a contributor than as the Bid Manager. However, he had managed smaller bids and had also had some sales training so he was considered a good choice for this prospect.

PROBLEM

Being experienced in delivery, Brian was very careful to make sure that the proposal included a workable solution. One of the deliverables required by the client was a risk analysis with particular emphasis on how the transition from the existing supplier to the new one would be handled. After all, for the financial institution continuity of service definitely came under the heading of 'mission critical'.

The company had a well-established risk management process based upon impact and probability, and Brian conscientiously followed this. The resulting risk analysis and plan covered all aspects of delivering the solution needed to meet the customer requirements. The problem was that this thorough risk analysis was focused on the delivery of the service to the client. However, it did not cover any risks relating to the procurement process itself. In particular it did not have an identified risk relating to the financial soundness of the customer. There had been a number of articles in the press and on television financial news suggesting that the next set of financial figures would show larger than expected losses. The customer's market sector was one that had seen a shake-out of smaller companies and mergers amongst medium-sized ones.

OUTCOME

The customer was the subject of a non-hostile takeover bid from one of its competitors. Consequently, the procurement was 'put on hold' by the client the day after the merger was announced. It would take the new company some time to come to grips with what infrastructures, commitments to existing suppliers, and premises it had. Until that happened there was little point in them going forward with the procurement. If this risk had been identified and assessed as being both medium to high probability and high impact it would have been possible to determine if it was a bid worth going on with.

LESSON LEARNT

Although considerable effort went into assessing the risks that would be involved in delivering the project, little or none had gone into looking at the bid itself. Consequently, when the procurement was suspended whilst the merger took place, the company had spent significant effort on a bid that might have been used elsewhere to greater effect. This is not a clear-cut, right and wrong, situation. It should be kept in mind that the outsourcing company had made an excellent job of the bid to shortlist and would undoubtedly stand a good chance of being considered for future business by the new organization. However, the key point is that this was a risk taken by default; nobody had consciously taken the decision that it was worth bidding for 'market presence' or the chance of future business after the merger. The lesson learnt is that the Bid Manager needs to make sure that risks relate to the bid itself, not just the solution.

Checklist

Item	Description	Completed?
Formal methods	Are you required to use a formal risk method (of your own or the client)? If so, have you the information needed to do so? Are you able to follow it?	
Risk identification	Have you attempted to identify all the risks? Have you involved all the people who can contribute to this (possibly including the client)? Have you chosen the best method?	
Risk register for bid	Have you produced one?	
Risk register – supplier	Have you produced one? Have you circulated it to the right people?	
Risk register – client	Does the client require one? If so, have you produced one? If not, would it be a useful sales tool? Has it been approved for submission to the client? Have you submitted it to the client?	
Risk assessment	Have all risks been assessed? Have the results been circulated, provided to those making any bid/no bid decisions?	
Risk plan	Does it cover all of the medium to high risks?	
Risk monitoring	Have you a process in place to keep a check on the risks? When there is a change are risks re-evaluated?	

5 Administration and Logistics

An administration, like a machine, does not create. It carries on. (St Exupery, 1942)

A significant fraction of the workload on any bid is in the sheer logistics of it all. Large quantities of information and paper need to be martialled, as do significant production jobs for internal and customer delivered drafts and documents. In addition to this there will be countless internal and customer meetings, not to mention being a channel for communication between all parties working on the bid. Overall this adds up to a big deal for the Bid Manager. Being aware of this, and what you have to handle is important if you are going to keep it under control. On very large bids there may be the luxury of an administrative resource to help with this, but it is often the case that it will fall to the Bid Manager to fulfil this role unaided. This does not mean the Bid Manager is there to be a dogsbody, but it does mean being responsible for making sure there is someone to get the jobs done.

In some ways there is an overlap between the administration and logistics activities defined here and the planning information provided in Chapter 6. This is because these activities do need to be planned for. However, it is possible to take these administrative activities in isolation and use them as the basis for a bid administrator's role. Whether you plan for them or not, these activities are essential if a bid is to be produced.

Figure 5.1 *Mind Map®: Administration and logistics*

This section highlights all the administrative jobs that need to be done in a typical bid. These include managing the bid file and associated correspondence, administering staff, office and technology resources; supporting and facilitating meetings; ensuring information is distributed; managing production of bid drafts and customer documents; controlling access to sensitive information, producing induction packs and so on. Although a checklist is provided at the end of the chapter, in some ways the whole chapter is a checklist and the would-be Bid Manager is encouraged to read it all to increase the chances of thinking of everything that needs to be looked after.

The Mind Map® in Figure 5.1 shows the relationship between the elements of this chapter. There is a considerable degree of interdependency between the administration and logistics involved in producing a bid.

> *Key point.* Minor administrative errors can have a major impact on a bid if they crop up at a critical moment. For example, forgetting to order a spare toner cartridge for a printer takes but a moment; trying to find a spare at 20.00 hours when everyone has gone home is a major event that can take all night.

Bid file

This is put first because, as an administrative activity, it is key to the success of the bid. It is a major administrative activity to maintain a complete and effective bid file. This is simply a central, and definitive, collection of the information relating to the bid. It is very important that this file is maintained as not only does it provide a central repository of information, but it also forms the basis for the handover to whomever has to implement the bid once the business is won. Even when a bid is lost the information in the bid file should be kept, at least for reference in future dealings with the same client. It can also act as a reference to refer to when working on similar bids. This is valuable information that should not be lost to the company.

These are the contents of a typical bid file:

No.	Title	Description
1	Correspondence in	Copies of all documents/letters/faxes, emails/phone call notes relating to bid in reverse date order, i.e. most recent at the front. This is in addition to any departmental filing (i.e. day file etc.).
2	Correspondence out	As above, but outgoing.
3	Meeting notes/minutes	Details of formal/informal meetings with clients and suppliers, internal or external, bid review meetings, etc.
4	Pre-qualifier, RFI, ITT, operational requirement (OR), Best And Final Offer (BAFO) and so forth	Reference copies of all formal tender-related documentation issued by the customer, preferably both paper and electronic copies.
5	Bid brief	Master copy of each issued bid brief (most recent at front).
6	Bid/project plans	Copies of any plans relating to the bid/the service to be delivered and the proposed solution. Most recent first. Copies of relevant sales and/or account plans.
7	Costing/pricing	Costing/pricing information/models.
8	Bids/proposals as delivered	Master copies of responses to pre-qualifiers, ITTs, ORs, invitation to negotiation (ITN), BAFO and so on.

9	Commercial	Terms and conditions, draft contracts and supporting schedules and so forth.
10	Third party information	Information received from third party/partner organizations, e.g. brochures, copy for proposals, etc. Where many third parties are involved the section can be subdivided as necessary.
11	Quality assurance (QA) and approvals	Copies of quality-related documents such as quality plans, accreditation certificates that apply, etc.
12	Risk	Information relating to risk assessment, management and control (e.g. risk register), issue logs and similar material.

Documentation

In addition to creating and keeping a bid file a regime needs to be set up to cover all the project documentation. This will include the drafts and final version of the bid itself, and any documentation that isn't already covered by the bid file. It is sensible to identify any standards that need to be applied to documentation. These may exist already, in which case use them unless they are really appalling; it will be a waste of time to start it from scratch. It is useful to have any template documents in place before work commences, it is a painful, and time-consuming business to apply them after the event.

Issue control (how a document's history and release is managed) is a difficult subject when it comes to bids. The author has seen staff used to an environment with formal change control reduced to gibbering wrecks by what goes on within the average bid. The pace of change does not permit any change request, change approval, document history or issue control to be applied to the majority of bid documents. The Bid Manager must come up with a pragmatic solution to this problem and negotiate with the powers that be any necessary exceptions from formal standards if the bid is to make headway. It is suggested that individual authors are encouraged to look after their own contributions on a day-to-day (or hour-to-hour!) basis. These can then be submitted to the Bid Manager when a draft of the bid is to be issued to a wider audience for review or to the client. Any formal issue control need then be applied to the whole document, not the rapidly changing components. A bid is always 'work in progress' until it is issued, as 'Version 1.0' to the client.

> *Key point.* With documentation the Bid Manager's motto should be, 'less is more'. This should be tempered with the requirement to make sure that everything vital is captured somewhere and that its location is known.

Distribution

Paper is something that proliferates in bids – drafts of drafts of drafts, not to mention all the official documents from the client, minutes of meetings and internal forms. Emails also tend to proliferate. It is up to the Bid Manager to make sure that all this ends up being seen by who needs to see it and to make sure that copies are kept for future reference. The Bid Manager also needs to make sure, or try to, that information does not get to those who should not see it.

One way of supporting this in very large bids, with multiple partner companies and so on is to set up, and maintain, formal distribution lists (electronically for email) that people can use to ensure consistency.

Confidential information

The Bid Manager and the bid team will inevitably have access to commercially sensitive information. In the case of government procurements there may well be classified, for example Restricted, Confidential and Secret (or above), information involved. Either way it will be up to the Bid Manager to make sure that the administration in place caters for this. In the case of government classified information then there will be specialist requirements. It is not within the scope of this book to deal with this, but Bid Managers should expect to cope with whatever is required, and may need an appropriate level of clearance to do the job.

Risk register(s)

It is normally part of a Bid Manager's job to maintain the risk register relevant to the bid (see Chapter 4 which covers risk and risk management). There may well be more than one of these registers. For example, there may be one for the bid, one for the project/services to be delivered and another for presentation to the client. It will normally fall to the Bid Manager to arrange for the administration of these documents. The example below is an extract from a typical risk register for a bid. See Chapter 4 for a description of risk management within the bid environment.

Risk ID	Description	Impact	Prob.	Contingency plan/owner	Date
	External				
1	Legislation may change affecting working hours in the UK. Would not affect European elements of bid.	M	M	No action, monitor risk.	12/6/06
2	Changes to scope of procurement. Would affect all bidders equally.	M	M	No action, monitor risk.	12/6/06

> *Note.* Where there is a separate project manager who is/would become responsible for client delivery once the bid has been won, this person may be responsible for the relevant risks. Where this is the case, it is essential that the Bid Manager and the project manager keep the registers in step, as there will be overlap.

In organizations that operate formal methods such as PRINCE 2 there may well be other registers and logs in addition to the risk register. What has been said here will apply equally to such information as far as administration goes.

Back-up policies

The Bid Manager must make sure that key files and documents are maintained in more than one place, ideally on a daily basis, particularly during periods of rapid change in the bid content, and on a separate site, but at least in a different part of the building or stored on a corporate/central computer system which is backed up in this way. Where documents are available only as paper copy, then photocopies should be taken as appropriate. Bids are produced in fast-moving, relatively high-pressure environments and there is little time for the recovery of lost information, it is vital that back-ups be done as quickly as possible.

Another useful point to consider is an audit trail. Rather than people constantly editing the same documents as they go along, losing previous versions/changes, it is a good idea that previous versions are kept for the duration of the bid. This may mean wasting space and keeping both electronic and paper copies of early drafts, but it can pay dividends on two fronts. First, ideas that were discarded in the early stages are often resurrected later on – this is useful information. If you have a copy of what was written or designed before, it can save time if it has to be written again. Second, documents and computer systems can pick up viruses; being able to go back to go back to an electronic copy which is a few days old and pre-virus and then update this from later paper copies is much easier than having to key in the whole document from scratch.

> *War Story*. The author knows of at least one example where the master copy of a proposal was lost to a computer crash the day before a bid was due to go out. Fortunately a version that was only a few days old and a hard copy of the final draft were to hand. It still took some hours to reconstruct the file, resulting in an overnight print and production run.

Meetings

For a complex, or even a relatively simple, bid there will be a requirement to hold a significant number of meetings. These will cover such things as sales plans, solution definition, weekly updates, bid approval, proposal reviews, analysis of customer documents and requirements. A large amount of a Bid Manager's time will be spent in arranging and helping with such meetings. Considerable time is wasted in bids where meetings descend into talking shops where the original point of the meeting gets forgotten because there is no agenda, or one of the key attendees is missing. As stated, a major goal of a Bid Manager is to avoid time being wasted as it is the most critical resource.

The administrative tasks for the Bid Manager relating to meetings include:

Location and facilities	Make sure rooms get booked, block book in advance for regular meetings such as weekly progress. If for a presentation or rehearsal, make sure that all the necessary equipment is available.
Agenda	Even if the Bid Manager is not running the meeting, or even involved, check that there is an agenda and that it is circulated in advance. For ad hoc meetings it is recommended that the first thing done is to agree on the agenda.
Invitation	Make sure that all attendees know in advance the when, where and the agenda. Set a good example for all meetings the Bid

	Manager runs. Make sure that essential attendees can be there, or reschedule.
Minutes/records	Whilst formal minutes of every meeting are neither appropriate nor needed, every meeting should result in a list of actions, with time limits that can be followed up. The Bid Manager must make sure that this happens and that a copy is available for the file. Failure to do this can result in chaos.
Actions	If there are no minutes then the Bid Manager should make sure that any actions allocated are recorded, communicated to the person given the action, and accepted by that person.

Note: the Bid Manager's job is to make sure these things happen, not necessarily to actually do the work.

CO-ORDINATION OF CLIENT MEETINGS

Another administrative role that is both necessary and beneficial is that of co-ordinating meetings with the client. This is particularly important where the bid team includes members from different organizations, for example in a consortium or partnership bid. There will be a number of fact-finding and exploratory meetings that people wish to have with the client. Obviously, if the same person in the client organization gets asked to three meetings that turn out to be to gathering much the same information then a degree of irritation will occur. They will see the supplier as disorganized and even as a threat to the bid because of the client's time that has been wasted. Remember, the client is also under pressure during a bid. So, to improve the chances of success it is sensible to co-ordinate these meetings. Either the Bid Manager should act as the single channel for organizing meetings with the client or all meeting requests must be arranged in consultation with the Bid Manager as the only person knowing what has been arranged and with whom. To this end the Bid Manager will need to know what the meeting is for, who it needs to be with and the proposed agenda.

> *War story.* The bid in question was to a large government department from a computer manufacturer in partnership with two other companies. The problem turned out to be with the operating divisions within the computer manufacturer. At one point the client complained that it felt it was dealing with six companies, not three. 'Would you please arrange it so that we only need to supply the same information no more than three times!' A certain amount of apologizing and grovelling was required, together with a concerted effort to co-ordinate meetings.

Resources

STAFF

In this case staff means the combination of full-time, part-time and third party staff that go to make up the bid team, plus any additional staff used for reviewing and approving the bid. It can be surprising to some people just how many staff become involved in even quite a small bid. Making sure that all these people are briefed and kept up to date is a significant task. In addition, it is often necessary to keep these individuals' management up to date in terms of their staff's involvement in the bid to make sure that the resource does not suddenly get double-booked and/or become unavailable to the bid team. This can be a major issue in organizations where multiple bids are happening at any given time, as there will be significant pressure on specialist resources.

The Bid Manager is responsible for making sure that all these people know what they are supposed to be doing, and when. In addition the Bid Manager must make sure that they have the physical resources available to them in order to get the job done.

INDUCTION

For staff joining the bid an induction pack is a good way of bringing them up to speed. Consistent with our overall theme, an induction packs saves time – the scarcest resource. Such a pack should include the following items:

Bid brief	A copy of the bid brief as described in this chapter. This provides a good level of background knowledge to the bid.
Reference material	Any draft documents, client literature that is helpful. Relevant standards, copies of previous bids that met similar requirements. Technical literature.
Contact list	Telephone, email, post, fax, mobile as appropriate for anyone involved in the bid.
Health and safety	Any health and safety information relating to the site, for example fire exits, first aid staff.
Terms of reference	Definition of what is to be done, who to report to, role and responsibilities.
Administrative	Email account, passwords, security badges, car park pass, etc.
Necessities	Where the coffee machines, lavatory, post room, lifts, nearest pub and restaurant, transport, parking, etc. are located. Desk, stationery and other items.

> *Note.* In this section it is only the administration of staff resources that is considered – the identification of appropriate resources is covered in Chapters 2 and 10.

SPACE AND EQUIPMENT

Even if the bid team is distributed throughout an organization it will need space in which to store information, have meetings and produce the physical proposal. The Bid Manager should take responsibility for identifying the physical space requirements, including filing cabinets, desk space and so forth. Do not underestimate the amount of time and effort that will be taken up in organizing and administering these resources, particularly in the early stages when the bid team is starting up. There can be a considerable amount of paperwork to process just to get a telephone line installed in a large organization. Even moving desks round to make a more productive space may not be trivial. There may be health and safety regulations that prevent staff from doing this themselves and it may take days to organize the appropriate support staff to get the job done. Remember lack of time is the bid team's greatest enemy. The sooner the paperwork gets moving the better.

> *Note.* In many cases it is valuable to have a dedicated bid room which is available for ad hoc meetings, keeping confidential information and generally acting as the headquarters for the bid team. This room should be connected to corporate services such as networks and phone lines. Ideally it should be close to the coffee machine.

PRODUCTION FACILITIES

Although this will vary from organization to organization, the Bid Manager should take responsibility for ensuring that all the equipment needed to produce the bid is available as and when required. Even when there is an administrative resource available to support the bid the Bid Manager should make sure that the resource has access to, and control over, what is required.

Equipment to consider includes:

Photocopiers	These will get used a great deal when distributing hard copy draft documents, and may be required for final production. If so, make sure that they have enough capacity, have been serviced, and that there is access to more than one of them at critical times. Make standby arrangements with an outside bureau.
Colour and black and white printers	It is vital that these not only have sufficient capacity to cope with any final print run but also that there are spares available in the form of back-up printers, toner and ink cartridges, paper, etc.
Hole punches	Of good quality and sufficient capacity to do the job required of them.
Staplers	Of good quality and sufficient capacity to do the job required of them.
Binders	Again, any binding and finishing technology used should be up to the job. Also make sure that more than one person knows how to use them.

SUPPORTING TECHNOLOGIES

This includes Internet and intranet access and connection to any internal databases and similar information. Although often outside the direct control of the Bid Manager, it is up to the Bid Manager to ensure that all who need access to such facilities can do so. Typically this will mean that, particularly for temporary and external staff, the Bid Manager will have to pass a request through an internal process for passwords and account names and so on.

EMAIL

As with the supporting technologies that may be required, the Bid Manager also needs to make sure that everyone who needs email has it. In most cases this means everyone who works on the bid! Again, this will require some amount of form filling. Also, the Bid Manager needs to make sure that the client has been informed of the email addresses of anyone they need to contact, and client email addresses need to be maintained.

Hint. Denial of service attacks on companies and those who provide email services are now quite common. If this happens at a critical part of a bid, for example when a proposal is being assembled with contributions from subcontractors, it can have serious consequences. It is worthwhile having alternative, stand-alone access to the outside world via email. For security and virus reasons this should be via a computer which is isolated from the organization information technology infrastructure. It may simply be the Bid Manager's home PC. The author has been in this situation – the organization involved was disconnected from the Internet for two days.

DELIVERY

Last, but by no stretch of the imagination least, is delivering the bid to the client. This may sound trivial, but it is often a cause of mad panic in many organizations that realize they have managed to produce the bid with 30 minutes to spare but have only just realized that one copy of the bid has to be delivered over a hundred miles away. This has happened, so be warned. This is one piece of logistics that you absolutely have to get right. Do not leave this until the last day to organize – you may find that there is no courier available, or you may notice too late that there is a requirement for delivery to a distant site. You will need to know from the courier or the delivery company what is the latest time that they can collect from you in order to deliver to the client before the deadline. If you are dealing with an international bid you may need to allow more than a day for delivery. If this looks like being a major problem for whatever reason, it is worth asking the client if an electronic copy, followed slightly later by a physical one will allow the deadline to be met.

> *Hint.* It is better to have a courier service deliver the bid than to use the company's staff. With a courier you will be able to obtain proof of dispatch and obtain a guarantee that it should be delivered on time. If it fails to get there on time most clients will accept that this was not your fault and will still accept that the bid has met their deadline. If you use company employees and their car breaks down then the matter is not so clear cut and there is a greater chance that your bid may be excluded.

CASE STUDY

SITUATION

Karl K was given the job of Bid Manager for a 'small to medium'-sized bid with a value of about £850 000 for the process control manufacturer for which he worked. Karl's 'day job' was as a production manager. As such he was often responsible operationally for high values of business. However, in this 'day job' he had access to a support office with administrative and technical support staff who dealt with the routine work. His usual role was to be on hand to solve operational problems and to report on how well the operation was running from week to week and from month to month. He had been seconded to run the bid, which was expected to take about two months, leaving his second in command to act as production manager with back-up support from Karl as needed. He would not be taking any of his support staff with him to assist with the bid.

PROBLEM

Karl was a good problem solver but, because

of the support usually available to him in his operational role, he had little exposure to administrative issues. Consequently, he underestimated the amount of time that would be required in the mechanics of producing large documents for review and final publication. He read the invitation to tender and supporting requirements documents and was quickly able to determine which parts he could deal with himself and which parts needed to be answered by other people within the company. His company knowledge and good reputation got things moving in the right direction with everyone committed to doing their bit. However, when it came to the last few days of the bid and Karl received everyone's contributions it became apparent that there was an awful lot of paper to be processed. Worse, there was only Karl available to process it. The final bid document came together on the Friday evening, and Karl got it priced up and approved for submission by the board. The bid was due in at 09.00 on Monday. He thought he was finished and would have no problems in meeting this date. Then he started to print, collate and bind the 14 copies, with separate pricing and technical annexes, brochures, annual reports and product specifications that the client demanded.

OUTCOME

The bid was delivered on time, just, but Karl worked a 36-hour stretch to complete it. He then drove this round to the client as, under pressure, he had forgotten to book a courier. Arguably this was a very high-risk solution as if he had had an accident then the bid would not have been delivered and all would have been in vain. As it happened the offices to which the bid needed to be delivered were actually on his way home (to sleep!) and only a short drive away. Shortly after this Karl came down with the flu, probably because his immune system would have been weakened by fatigue, and the cost to the company of this time off was much greater than the cost of administrative

support would have been. Admittedly this is less disastrous than if he had fallen asleep at the wheel of the car, but it was not an ideal result.

LESSON LEARNT

The main lesson learnt by Karl was not to underestimate just how much administrative and production work is involved in delivering a bid. This is doubly true in any government-related work or for large organizations with established and bureaucratic procurement systems. The use of a relatively inexpensive support staff to cope with the burdens of running a bid of this nature would have been an excellent investment. The end product would have been better produced, increasing the chances of winning. More time would have been available to focus on the profitability of the business. Karl would not have been off sick and would not have ended up driving when so tired that he might have been injured or prosecuted if an accident had occurred.

Checklist

Item	Description	Completed?
Resource – staff	Have they all been briefed? Induction packs? Allocated passwords for email access where needed? Allocated a desk and a phone? Health and safety information?	
Meetings	Meeting room Time and date Attendees informed Agenda Minutes/notes Actions follow-up	
Documentation	Filing? Distribution? Templates?	
Confidential information	Are sufficient security procedures in place for the nature of the information used in the bid? Is commercially sensitive information protected from competitors?	

Bid file	Have you got one? Is it accessible? Is it secure?	
Back-ups	What procedures are in place to ensure that the bid is safe? Are off-site copies of data, photocopies of key documents and so forth being kept up to date?	
Email and Internet/ intranet	Distribution lists? Access?	
Production equipment	Is all the equipment required available? For example: (a) Photocopiers (b) Printers (c) Binders, staplers, hole punches (d) Stock of paper (e) Spare toner/ink for printers (f) Space for collation and binding (g) Packing materials	
Delivery	Has the courier been booked and is the courier reliable? Do you have a plan B in case you miss the deadline for the courier (for example email)?	

6 *Planning*

Adventure is the result of poor planning. (Colonel Blatchford Snell)

A key element of successful bid management is planning. This does not mean that the production of complicated project network diagrams or highly detailed 'micro-management' plans are required. Pragmatism is the essence of planning for bids. By its nature the bid environment is highly changeable – the client may suddenly request a new requirement to be included, sales may identify a different approach that requires work to be reviewed and so on. It is not practical to maintain a plan at the detail level for a bid, nor is it desirable as the manager would be spending all the available time updating the plan rather than doing useful work. All that is needed is a plan that defines the major milestones and who is responsible for delivering what, in other words, who does what, where and when. This chapter will help with this by identifying what is likely to need doing and how long it may take.

The Mind Map® in Figure 6.1 shows how the topics in planning are linked. For clarity not all activities discussed have been included. The key point is that there is a significant level of interaction between all the elements of the plan which will be in a continual state of change during the bid.

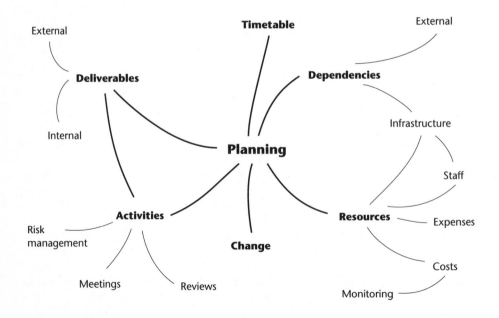

Figure 6.1   *Mind Map®: Planning*

Timetable

A key differentiator between the world of the Bid Manager and the world of the project manager is that the timetable has been fixed, together with the major milestone dates, before you start to plan. On the plus side this actually simplifies matters considerably as you have one less variable to consider. On the minus side it means that you are constrained as to what you can achieve in the timetable, regardless of how much resource is available to you; the analogy being with that of the number of men you can have digging a hole – there is only so much space available to dig in. Your 'hole' is defined by the timetable for each stage of the bid process.

There is sometimes scope for negotiating extensions to the customer's timetable. Indeed, they may extend it themselves because they need to make changes to their requirements or cannot support the procurement on the original schedule. However, it is always a sensitive issue from a sales viewpoint. If your organization is the only one asking for a delay, then it suggests that you are not as efficient as your competitors. As the Bid Manager your goal must be to keep to the timetable. If you do really think that it is impossible, and have a good reason why, then the sooner you inform the sales function the better. They can then have off-the-record conversations to either lay the ground for an extension based upon a good reason or to test the client's reaction to such changes.

The overall timetable for the type of bid that this book addresses varies from a few weeks to about a year. This will be split between an initial questionnaire aimed at producing a shortlist, a proposal in response to a detailed set of requirements and a final negotiation aimed at selecting the final winner.

> *Note to management.* The timetable is always tight. In many organizations even though people know the bid is coming in nothing is done until the paperwork arrives. Then it sits around on someone's desk for a couple of days before action is taken. The result, a short timetable becomes almost impossible, everyone works through the night and a poor job is done. Do not let this happen in your organization – if you know a bid is happening, give it an owner before it arrives.

Deliverables

For a bid the deliverables come in two categories: client and internal – those that have to be delivered to the client and those that need to be produced to satisfy the organization that the bid should go ahead.

CLIENT

The client deliverables will be, as a minimum, a description of what is to be supplied and the price for supplying it. In addition there may be a requirement to produce supporting information, a risk register, pricing of options, special terms and conditions, risk/reward sharing schemes, customer references, financial statements, responses to mandatory and desirable requirements, and so on.

The contents of a typical bid document are (you will need someone to deliver each part):

1   Introduction;
2   Management summary;
3   Understanding of requirement;
4   Proposed solution;
5   Response to requirements (for example mandatory and desirable requirements);
6   Financial proposal (prices and payment options);
7   Annexes (brochures, annual reports, technical specifications, quality certificates and so forth).

INTERNAL

The internal deliverables will also be organization specific. Typically they will include a case for bidding and internal approval, plus sufficient documentation to support the delivery of what has been sold. These deliverables will account for the bulk of the creative work that has to be done by the bid team and any suppliers and partners involved.

RESPONSIBILITY

It is imperative that for every deliverable identified there is an individual person or organization that is responsible for it. This is a key job for the Bid Manager that must be made a high priority during the early stages of the bid. Furthermore, it is not enough to identify who does what, it is also essential to get their confirmation that they can do it and within the timetable.

Activities

There is a wide range of activities that crop up during a bid, for example industry-specific activities such as compliance with regulatory authorities, monopolies and mergers issues, specific technical requirements and so on, and they cannot all be covered here. However, all bids require certain generic activities to be completed, and points to consider relating to these are given below in order to help with planning. There may be more, or less, in a particular bid but this list will get you started, particularly if this is a first time.

START-UP

All bids should include a start-up, or kick-off, meeting where the principal members of the bid team get together to discuss the bid and agree a common understanding and approach. This meeting should be held within the first week after receiving the ITT or whatever formal documentation you are supplied with by the client to initiate the bid.

> *Hint.* If you know about a bid before the client sends you the documentation, and you probably will if you are to have a good chance of winning, then set up a bid awareness meeting and present an overview of what is expected. This gives people due warning and allows them to plan ahead, improving the chances of you getting the necessary resource on time.

PLANNING AND ADMINISTRATION

As stated in the roles and responsibilities chapter, a significant part of a Bid Manager's time will be spent on administrative tasks. Plan for this as time is especially important where the Bid Manager has a second role, for example is also the sales person or the project manger who will deliver the solution/services/product to the client after the bid is won.

INFRASTRUCTURE

Consideration must be given to how long it will take to get things set up to enable the bid team to work effectively. In some organizations this may be trivial. For example, there may be a dedicated bid production facility and a meeting room that can be booked for the team's use for the duration of the bid, and the team members may already have all the equipment, information technology and so on that they will need. In other organizations, particularly those that do not get involved in major bids on a regular basis, it may be necessary to set up everything from scratch, a significant undertaking that must be planned for. In most cases the reality will be somewhere in between. The author has often had to spend time getting equipment moved and set up, often a time-consuming activity in a large company.

> *Hint*. Where bureaucracy and/or internal complexities are great it may be worth setting up a small, dedicated set of basic equipment that is not connected to any corporate infrastructure, solely for the use of the team. The cost of this can often be justified in terms of time and effort saved.

RISK

Risk assessment and planning will be significant in supporting the decisions that have to be made during the bid process. It is necessary to plan time to do this. During the life of the bid, risks should be reviewed at least once a week. Chapter 3 on methods and approaches describes the risk management process in sufficient detail for planning purposes if the reader is not already familiar with it.

UPDATE MEETINGS

These should be held as often as is needed, as some flexibility is desirable. It is suggested that once a week should be adequate, more often than that and the overhead of the meetings becomes an issue. The plan should allow for the time that these meetings may take.

APPROVAL MEETINGS

The frequency of these will vary from organization to organization but there ought to be one in advance of every customer deliverable document. These meetings will require more advance notice because they will usually involve senior staff on the approval side who will not be available at short notice. It is a good idea to schedule these as soon as you get the timetable for the bid from the client, but keep in mind that fate will undoubtedly intervene. These meetings also require considerable preparation and briefing support for the attendees who will not be as familiar with the bid as the team are; in many cases it is similar to briefing a Red team (see Chapter 3).

SUBCONTRACTOR MEETINGS

Again these will vary in frequency and formality according to the relationship with the subcontractor. They are much the same as other meetings, but there may be planning issues relating to location and travel and these need to be taken into account. There may also be a requirement for non-disclosure agreements and the like which will increase the overall time needed for the initial meetings.

> *Note.* In some cases the same subcontractor may be bidding with more than one prime contractor. If this is the case, be careful what you disclose and listen for hints as to the opposition's plan.

REVIEWS AND RED TEAM MEETINGS

Planning for a review meeting includes:

- making the material to be reviewed available in sufficient time for the reviewers to read it;
- providing a brief for the reviewers that makes it clear what they are to review for;
- booking rooms for meetings and discussions;
- making sure there is a forum for reviewers' comments to be given back to the bid team.

Chapter 3 on methods and approaches goes into detail on the function of Red team reviews.

PRODUCTION

Do not underestimate the time that will be taken up in the physical production and publication of any customer deliverable document. This also applies to drafts of such documents for internal review. You must allow for all the separate contributions to be edited into a common document, or set of documents. Make sure that there is enough time for printing, punching, collating and binding.

> *War story.* One of the author's clients had a major problem with the production element of bids. They did not have any dedicated facilities, in fact people producing the bids had to beg, borrow and steal practically everything they needed. The frustrated Bid Managers had even gone to the trouble of getting the local stationery supplier to stock special binders for them as they could not guarantee supply internally. They always worked through the night to produce their bids, in one case the team had worked for 38 hours without sleep. Most of this time was spent in making up for the shortcomings such as access to a working photocopier, only one colour printer and that was only available when not being used by marketing, no stationery cupboard on site so that running out of paper was a real issue. As you can imagine, these people did not feel that the company was on their side.

There is an argument often put forward by sales people that, 'if we aren't producing the document at the last minute then we have wasted time that could have been used making a better sales case in the proposal'. This is a specious argument; the proposal should document the sales case that has already been put forward to the client by the sales force, and there should not be any surprises or new approaches in it. It is important that the delivered documents represent the case well and give a professional impression of the supplier. You can only achieve this by making sure there is time to check and produce the deliverable documentation in a calm manner. There is no value in having to work through the night; it does not mean you are dedicated to your job, although some people think there is some sort of machismo in doing so, it just means you are inefficient. Having received bids as well as produced them, you can tell which ones were produced 10 minutes before the deadline.

> *Hint.* If there are sections that need to be created or changed at the last minute, structure the document so that these are stand-alone sections. Then you can produce the rest of the document, proof it and check it in relative calm.

POST-BID ACTIVITIES

It is often overlooked that there is a need for a significant amount of activity after the bid has been won or lost. The plan should include time for this. Typical activities include a post-bid review meeting with the client and the internal team to look at lessons learnt, and hand-over meetings to those who have to deliver the solution once the business has been won.

Dependencies

Normally a major element of any project plan is what has to happen first before a particular activity can start. The conventional approach to project planning is to identify the activities first, then the dependencies so that you can identify a sequence of events. This is usually represented as either a network diagram, such as a PERT chart or a bar chart (for example, Gantt) that shows how the activities relate to each other. This is then fleshed out by the addition of time taken and resources involved to produce a plan. For a bid this is interesting, but not really that helpful. The essence of running a bid is for everything to be happening as fast as it can – the real dependencies will be at a high level. For example, when does the client issue the requirements, when do you have a solution, when do you have a price? Any dependencies at a lower level need to be resolved by communication. This works because the deliverables within a bid have relatively short times associated with them. The raw materials are people's thoughts and ideas not long lead time items. Consequently, there is no need for complex, and with the level of change and the short timetables, relatively meaningless dependency-driven plans.

> *Key point.* This does not mean you do not need to be aware of critical dependencies, such as non-availability of critical staff, production facilities and so on. But you must not waste time on details you cannot control.

Resources

This refers, specifically, to estimating how much resource and time will be needed to complete the bid. This should not be confused with estimating how much work, product and so on are needed to deliver whatever the client is trying to procure. This highlights another difference between bids and projects, which comes on the estimating side. With projects there will almost certainly be some attempt to split the work into its components in some form of work breakdown structure and to estimate the effort and resources required for each element. This will produce a resource plan for the project that can then be matched with available resources to produce a viable estimate of time to complete and resource utilization.

Sadly, this is not so easy for a bid – at least if you are after an accurate result. For one thing you will not be able to assess all the tasks involved that you will need in order to produce a detailed work breakdown structure (WBS). The scope of the work will change according to the solution to the client requirements that the bid team develop. Worse still, this solution will change in response to client, competitor and sales instigated events. In a bid change is endemic and rapid. In other words you do not really have a proper specification in the first place.

There is a pragmatic approach where you look at the overall timetable for the bid, as specified by the client, then make a first pass at the types of resources required, for example technical, commercial, sales and so on. Next assess how much of this is full time (100 per cent), how much is half time (50 per cent), and how much is quarter time (25 per cent). Anything less than one day a week can be safely ignored because there will be a fudge factor added that will cover it. You are now in a good position to make an educated guess by multiplying the resources need by the overall time of the bid by the percentage utilization. Next add 25 per cent to this to cover inevitable changes that will be introduced both by the client and the supplier organization and to cope with the small jobs that were deliberately left out.

Mathematically this can be expressed as $D_b = \sum R_n \times P_n \times T$ where D_b is the number of person days to deliver the bid, R_n are the individual resources, P_n is the percentage utilization for R_n and T is the expected duration of the bid.

In addition, any special equipment, office rental, delivery and production costs should be added, although these will usually be low in comparison to the staff costs. However, do not underestimate how long it can take to set up the infrastructure. In many organizations it is by no means trivial to get a desktop computer set up. It can take anything from days to weeks to get a PC delivered and configured.

Where a dedicated bid room (sometimes known as a war room) is being set up from scratch, the amount of effort and time involved will be significant.

For example, consider the case where NB plc is bidding for the supply of a transport and logistics service to an electrical retail company. The bid team consisted of a full-time Bid Manager, who was also the sales resource, a full-time logistics expert, a full-time technology specialist, together with three part-time (25 per cent) delivery managers and a part-time (50 per cent) administrator. The bid is to run for three months. This adds up to about 195 days of effort. In addition, senior management is planned to spend about 10 days in reviewing and approving the bid. This makes the total 205 days. It is suggested that this be done using a spreadsheet to make life easier (Figure 6.2). Alternatively a project management package can be used, which usually has the benefit of supporting the production of graphical displays of the project reports and so on.

Resource	Start date	End date	Utilization	Days	Subtotal
Bid Manager	2-Feb-06	2-May-06	100%	60	60
Administration	2-Feb-06	2-May-06	50%	30	30
Technical specialist	2-Feb-06	2-May-06	100%	60	60
Delivery manager 1	2-Feb-06	2-May-06	25%	15	
Delivery manager 1	2-Feb-06	2-May-06	25%	15	
Delivery manager 2	2-Feb-06	2-May-06	25%	15	45
Senior manager	3-Mar-06	2-May-06		10	10
			Total	205	

Figure 6.2   *Spreadsheet example of time required*

Costing

Related to estimating is costing, again this is the cost of the bid, not the cost of the products and services to be delivered to the client. This can be very difficult for bids as many of the costs are hidden. For example sales time is often considered as overhead. After all you cannot charge the client for it so why keep account of it? One good reason for so doing is that it provides useful information when it comes to deciding whether or not to continue with a bid.

Any special equipment, office rental, delivery and production costs should also be added, although these will usually be low in comparison to the people costs except when a dedicated facility is set up from scratch.

Taking our example above (NB plc is bidding for the supply of a transport and logistics service to an electrical retail company) there were 175 days of effort in total. If the senior management time were charged internally at £1000 per day, the specialist and sales resources at £500 per day and the administrator at £300 per day then the resource cost for the bid would be £101 500. These charges include the internal overhead of equipment supply, but not the consumables, couriers' fees incurred in delivering the bid, travelling to client meetings and so forth. The estimate for these was £2000. This gives a total estimated bid cost of £103 500. This is a significant cost which forms part of the opportunity cost of sale for the bid. In this case the total value of the business that NB plc were bidding for was £2.5 million, which makes the outlay seem worthwhile at first sight. However, if the expected margin on the business were to be only 15 per cent then the cost of sale would be a significant fraction of the expected margin. In this example the margin would be £375 000 so nearly a third of this would go in the bid cost. The spreadsheet example in Figure 6.3 shows how this could be automated – anything to save time!

As before, a project management package can be useful here as it can also do the sums for you. If you are familiar with one then this can be a time saver, if not the spreadsheet is probably quicker.

Key point. Because clients cannot be charged directly for bids and many of the costs are classed as overhead, it is quite common for costs to be ignored. This is a mistake as costing a bid, even at the simplest level of how many days of effort, provides essential planning information for deciding which bids to go for in the future. Indeed, when considering a bid/no bid decision, cost should be one of the deciding factors.

Resource	Start date	End date	Utilization	Days	Subtotal	Rate	Cost
Bid Manager	2-Feb-06	2-May-06	100%	60	60	£500	£30 000
Administration	2-Feb-06	2-May-06	50%	30	30	£300	£9 000
Technical specialist	2-Feb-06	2-May-06	100%	60	60	£500	£30 000
Delivery manager 1	2-Feb-06	2-May-06	25%	15			
Delivery manager 1	2-Feb-06	2-May-06	25%	15			
Delivery manager 2	2-Feb-06	2-May-06	25%	15	45	£500	£22 500
Senior manager	3-Mar-06	2-May-06		10	10	£1000	£10 000
			Total	205			£101 500
Expenses							
Travel							£2000
Total costs							£103 500

Figure 6.3 *Spreadsheet example of cost of time required*

MONITORING

If you are looking at costs it may be desirable to monitor them as the bid progresses. This is conventionally done when managing a project. However, whilst it is important not to let costs get out of control, a bid is not like a delivery project. The Bid Manager's prime responsibility is to get the bid, preferably with the strongest sales message possible, on time. The Bid Manager should not be aiming to get the job done under budget. There is an old adage that for any job you can only have two out of three of good, quick and cheap. The Bid Manager's jobs are always in the quick category, and hopefully in the good. So, whilst it is useful to keep a rough eye on costs versus estimate, if only to make sure you have a justification for any increased spend, do not spend too much time on it until after the bid has been delivered.

Sample plan

This example is based upon a plan actually used by the author. Only the names and times have been changed to protect the guilty and innocent alike. It worked sufficiently well to support a successful sales campaign.

EXAMPLE TIMETABLE

This plan is for a government department procurement and covers the period from the long list proposal through to the preparation of the BAFO. It is worth noting that the major milestones are client defined and that they, in combination with the time needed to manage reviews and the production of the deliverable documents, drive the rest of the plan.

This part of the plan was also summarized as follows (internal meetings are italicized):

Activity	Date
Issue requirement specification	14/5/05
Open meeting with client and competitors	08/6/05
Internal SWOT (strength, weakness, opportunity, threat) analysis	
Meeting with Subcontractor (re: partnering)	*10/6/05*
Bid approval meeting	*15/6/05*
RED TEAM DRAFT	18/6/05
RED TEAM REVIEW meeting	22/6/05
Receive proposals	25/6/05
Short list suppliers	16/7/05
Short list briefing – draft agreements issue	21/7/05
Supplier internal review agreement 0.1	26/7/05
V0.1 review – government client	30/7/05
V0.2 review – government client	Week 9/8/05
V0.3 review – government client	Week 30/8/05
V0.4 Review – government client	Week 20/9/05
Supplier presentations	Last two weeks 9/05
Reference site visits/supplier visits	09/05 and 10/05
Due diligence data requests	Mid 8/05 for 9/05
V0.5 review – government client	Week 04/10/05
V1.0 review – government client	Week 18/10/05
Formal agreement V1.0	Week 25/10/05
BAFO ITT	By 29/10/05
Tender required	By 9/11/05
Evaluation complete	By 12/11/05
Execute agreement	By 19/11/05

EXAMPLE ACTIVITIES

To support such a plan a variety of people needed to deliver their part of the bid and take responsibility for reviewing and approving it. A second summary was used that defined the who does what activity. This summary relates to the period from the issue of the short list to the Version 0.1 review with the client.

Note: the 'real' table covered a longer period and included more detail which has been left out for brevity.

What	Who	When
Comments on terms and conditions (TACs) plus Schedule 1	Legal Eagle	30/7/05
Schedule 2 – Produce rough draft	Bid Manager	30/7/05
Technology refresh	Technical Sales Support	30/7/05
Strategy	Technical Architect	30/7/05
Help desk	Delivery Manager	30/7/05
2 – Management structure	Delivery Manager	30/7/05
2 – Application development	Technical Sales Support	30/7/05
Maintenance	Delivery Manager	30/7/05
Technical platform	Technical Sales Support	30/7/05
Costing	Bid Team	28/7/05
Training	Training Manager	30/7/05
V0.1 agreement internal review	Bid Team	26/7/05
V0.1 Government client review	Bid Team	30/7/05

Change

Were this to be a book about project management, then there would be a whole chapter about change. This would cover sources of change, how impact is assessed, whether or not the change will be accepted and a whole raft of details concerning methodologies. For the Bid Manager change is a fact of life, the job is to juggle the activities required to deliver the bid. As discussed elsewhere, there is usually little that can be done to change the timetable and the evolutionary nature of the response to the bid change will be constant. As a Bid Manager the only thing to be done is to live with the level of change and to support the team in coping with it. This is not a normal project environment; there are no prizes for coming in under budget, only for winning the business.

CASE STUDY

SITUATION

Company A, which specialized in industrial catering and facilities management, had recently taken on a new sales person. Helen was very experienced in sales and had a good track record in winning business by coming up with creative solutions to customer problems. She was particularly good at building good relationships with the client and identifying what the real problems were. Her industry background was in supplying catering equipment, so she had good working knowledge of the clients of her new employer. However, her main skills were in negotiation and selling, not management.

This procurement, by a large manufacturing group with several premises, represented a significant increase in business for the group with a high-profile client. Consequently, this was business that would have both a financial and a public relations/market presence benefit.

PROBLEM

Although Helen had a good grasp of the sales and sales management environments she had only very limited project management knowledge, and mainly theoretical at that. Because of this she tended to concentrate on what the sales campaign was going to be, identifying the win strategy and lobbying decision makers and influencers in the client organization in an attempt to win the business. Her plan was limited to providing management with the top-level timetable for the bid and letting them know she would need certain specialists to write parts of the bid. Unfortunately she did not identify on a section-by-section basis who was going to write which part of the bid, neither did she put in any steps for reviewing the bid. The plan she issued, but only to her management is shown below (the items in italics are internal activities):

Activity	Who	Date
Receive invitation to tender	Helen	27/7/08
Analyse requirement	Technical specialists	28/8/08 to 21/9/08
Submit questions to client	Helen	22/8/08
Receive client answers	Helen	30/9/08
Develop solution and response	Technical specialists	22/8/08 to 11/9/08
Write proposal	Helen, Technical specialists	12/9/08 to 23/9/08
Submit proposal	Helen, Technical specialists	24/9/08
Supplier presentation	Helen, Technical specialists	3/10/08
Announcement of result	Helen	18/10/08

What it fails to do is make sure that there are no gaps and, because it only allows for a final draft, there is no scope for identifying these gaps until it is too late.

OUTCOME

Although the bid seemed to start well and Helen established a very good level of influence with the client, and indeed identified many factors that the client perceived as critical to their business, the inevitable happened. When the proposal started to come together it became clear that an important section of the bid, on health and safety policy, had been missed altogether. Furthermore, one department had thought they were not due to deliver their copy until the date the bid was due to go in. When it was reviewed it was found not to meet the client's requirements. There was now very little time to revise this work. Furthermore, even if these sections could be rewritten they would require the bid to be repriced, requiring still more last minute work.

The bid failed to complete on time, with just one hour to go new material was still being written and priced. Helen went to the client to ask for an extension but by then it was too late. The client knew that it would get enough bids from the competitors to make an informed decision. They reasoned that if they cannot get good service when you are trying to win business from them, what will it be like once you have won it?

LESSON LEARNT

Helen's inexperience of bid management meant that she had not understood how important it was to make sure everyone knew what they were supposed to be doing and by when. Having a simple plan, clearly communicated, would have saved a huge amount of turmoil, and might well have resulted in the delivery of a winning proposal. For most bids, even quite complex ones, the plan needs to be little more than a timetable and a list of who is delivering what. Complex PERT or Gantt charts are not required, and are seldom helpful.

Her employer also realized that it should sharpen up either its recruitment processes or make sure that it provided the relevant skills training to its staff so that they were able to do their jobs effectively. In their favour they did not sack Helen, but sent her on a basic project planning course.

Checklist

Item	Description	Completed?
Plan	Have you got a plan?	
Timetable	Is this clear and understood by team? Are resources committed? Are management aware of timetable?	
Deliverables	Are they all identified? Is someone identified as 'owning' each one?	
Dependencies	Are major dependencies identified (do not worry about the detail)?	
Who does what	Is this in sufficient detail? Are there any gaps? Are all resources identified?	
Distribution	Has the plan gone to all those who need it?	
Audit	Has receipt of the plan been acknowledged and the actions/timetable agreed to?	

Costs	Is there a cost plan? Have you recorded what you actually spent?	
Time	Are you sure you have allowed enough time for production?	

2 *Writing and Editorial*

Part 2: Summary

Part 2 covers the editorial, design and wordsmithing skills that are needed if the Bid Manager is responsible for the look, feel, consistency and written style of the finished product. These skills are sometimes delegated to a specialist proposal editor, bid production manager or technical writer. However, they are also useful for anyone who is involved in writing a section of a bid and so they are separated from the rest of the skills, in Part 3, for the convenience of the reader (Figure P.2). If the reader only learns the difference between a feature and a benefit then Part 2 will have made a positive contribution to the work done by anyone working on a bid. It is recommended that all three chapters are read to get the full picture and gain a good overall understanding of what goes into making a good-looking bid that reads well.

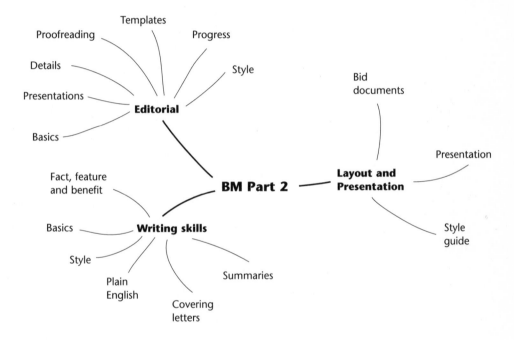

Figure P.2   *Mind Map®: Bid management, Part 2*

7 *Writing Skills*

Writing comes more easily if you have something to say. (Sholem Asch, 1955)

Writing skills matter; what you get away with in an email or a memo will not do in a bid or proposal. This chapter is aimed at all those who have to write contributions for a bid. Even if the contributor is used to producing a significant amount of written material such as reports, letters and so forth, there is a sales aspect to the content of a bid that requires special skills (Figure 7.1).

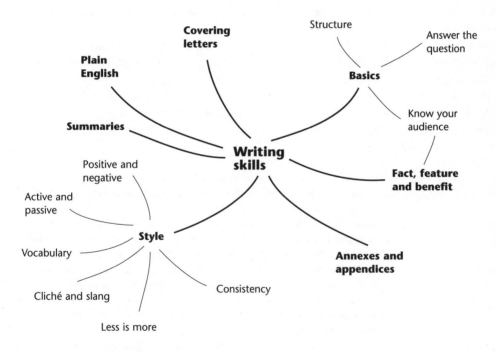

Figure 7.1 *Mind Map®: Writing skills*

The basics

In Part 3, there is a significant amount of information devoted to the gentle art of communication, and it won't do the reader any harm to look at Chapter 10 before setting fingers to keyboard. The most important element of this is *know your audience* and write for them. As a minimum the writer of any section of a bid document should consider this 'get you started' checklist:

Item	Completed?
Is the spelling correct?	
Is the grammar correct?	
Is it the right word, for example 'to' when you meant 'too'?	
Is there a summary at the start?	
Do you need a conclusion at the end? If so, do not put any new information in it.	
Are there any analogies that are likely to confuse the reader?	
Is all the information relevant to the reader and the subject?	
Can you usefully shorten any of the longer sentences?	

KNOW YOUR AUDIENCE

For a bid this is not so simple, different parts of the bid will be read by different audiences, and some parts will be read by multiple audiences who will have different, perhaps conflicting, requirements. For example, it is relatively easy to establish that a technical annex dealing with detailed information will mainly be of interest to other technical specialists. However, an overview of the proposed business solution may well need to be read by a mixed audience including financial, legal, operational, technical and management specialists.

Below is a list of the likely specialist readers of a bid and some, admittedly subjective, comments on what they might look for. These are the types of things that an author should be thinking about when planning what they are going to write. More senior staff are likely to look at the summary sections more than the detail parts of the bid. To this end, and to make sure that readers can gain an overall understanding of the bid, any specialist section should be prefaced with an introduction/summary that makes the section understandable to the general reader.

Senior management/ board level	Have limited time available so will need to be able to get what they need from any bid document quickly. As stated, good summary sections are a must. The management summary for the whole bid must meet this need.
Financial	Expect these readers to focus on what it is all going to cost. Also any impact the bid is likely to have on existing revenue and cost streams (for example, a bid for anything to do with infrastructure will have implications outside any direct costs).
Sales	The sales/sales management of the client will want to see how the bid will enable them to sell more/gain a competitive edge. These readers are strongly motivated and will probably look for little else. They are likely to read little more than summaries, as they are likely to be 'activist' in nature and want quickly to get their information.
Technical specialists	Will want to check that the technical information is correct. Will have own views on what the solution should be and, if the solution proposed is different, they will need to be convinced that it will work. They need to have a clear and complete description of what is being offered with sufficient technical detail to allow them to make such an assessment. It may be necessary to have very detailed information in separate annexes/appendices if space is at a premium in the main bid document. It is acceptable to use specialist language and jargon here, but it should still be explained in a glossary to make sure there is a common understanding of any terms and acronyms used.
Quality	By their nature these readers will be very detailed in their examination of a bid document. Within their own specialist section they will be looking for consistency and clear evidence that the subject of quality is understood. It

would be poor policy to gloss over the surface; you will need to provide evidence in depth. It may be necessary to include much of this in annexes (or appendices). They will point out if you have any errors you have in page numbering, dates, version numbers and the like. Get it right.

Human resources	Will be looking for any impact the bid will have on staff, both their own and in the bidding organization. They will be aware of legislation that relates to employment and health and safety at work. As with the technical and specialist readers it is acceptable to use specialist terms for these readers.
Purchasing	Mainly focus on getting the best deal. Will focus on anything that can be negotiated. Level of technical understanding varies with background and industry.
Project managers	As might be expected these people will be looking at the approach used for running the project/implementing the service and so on. They may have particular methods that they prefer – refer to them if possible. Will focus on how things are to be done more than why they are being done, not as benefit oriented as sales and general management.
Operations	Here the key interest will be in how what is bid will fit in with existing day-to-day operations.
Legal and commercial	Will mainly be checking terms and conditions and financial considerations. There will probably be a requirement to include draft contracts and payment schedules. These will need to be produced with the help of the appropriate specialist as legal terms have very specific meanings that may not be what they seem at first sight. Contract schedules and the like will need to be in their own section/annex if they are not going to spoil the flow of the main bid. Clients may well offer their own terms and conditions for consideration or completion as part of the bidding process. These people look at detail; it needs to be there.

Note. Irrespective of the role of the reader he or she will still have preferences and prejudices. It helps if the writer can find out about these if at all possible. For example, one of the evaluators of a bid the author worked on had very strict views about English usage and delighted in pointing out any errors he found in any document he received. He would even reply to emails pointing out the mistakes!

ANSWER THE QUESTION

A big part of any bid will be made up of answers to questions posed by the client. This needs to be looked on in much the same way as an examination question. The critical thing is to answer the question as asked within the context of the information supplied by the client. Read the question several times before beginning to write a response. If in any doubt ask someone else what they think it means. Only then set pen to paper or fingers to keyboard. Once an answer has been drafted, check it again against the original question. Where the client has provided an electronic copy of their questions it is a good idea to include the question in the bid document before the answer. This makes it easy for an evaluator to match the answer to the question. It also makes it easier for the writer, and later the editor or any internal reviewer, to see if the question has been answered. This may seem to be over-stressing this point, but experience shows that failing to answer the question is one of the most common faults in public sector bids.

Failing to answer the questions is one of the dangers of the uncritical use of 'boiler plate'.

Questions that look similar at first sight may turn out to be very different in detail and in context. It is very easy to reuse an answer from an earlier bid to a different client as it saves time. However, this answer may be inappropriate for the new client and may well damage the overall credibility of the bid.

Note. Many government procurements, and quite a few commercial ones, will have questions that are given a 'Mandatory' status. This means that they have to be answered with a compliant response. To provide this it is necessary to answer the question asked – not a similar one that might have been easier. Putting in the word 'compliant' will not do!

STRUCTURE

There are two elements to this: the structure of a document and the structure of a sentence.

When writing anything much longer than a paragraph it is a good idea to consider structure. For almost everything that will be included in a bid the following structure should work well:

Introduction	Say what you are going to say, introduce the topics that will be covered and the order in which they will be produced. This allows the reader quickly to decide if it is relevant to them and roughly where they will find out something they are specifically interested in.
Main paragraph(s)	It is a good idea to have a logical connection from one paragraph to the next. Most importantly do not put a paragraph in front of one that contains information that it will depend upon.
	Similarly the rule is that a paragraph only deals with one subject. If you find that after you have finished it you have covered more than one, split the paragraph up. *For example, 'This equipment processes potatoes in 30 per cent less time than competing equipment. Our in-house publications unit is expert in the production of training material'.* These points are not related and do not belong together. When this is done within the same sentence it is known as Zeugma: 'She went out of the room in tears and a sedan chair.'
Conclusion	Summarize the key points that have been made and show that they support any conclusions that you make. Do not introduce any new information in this section.

It is worth putting in the extra time needed to provide the introduction and the summary. Apart from getting the message across, it also provides a check that what you thought you meant is what you have actually written. If the conclusion is not supported by the main paragraphs then either the conclusion is wrong or something has been left out (or put in and should not have been).

With regard to sentence structure, assuming that you have a subject, verb and an object (The cat sat on the dog), be aware that word order changes meaning and emphasis. Read the following aloud.

- 'The Minister can't even understand statistics.'
- 'Even the Minister can't understand statistics.'

Only one word has been moved, but the meaning is very different. This can be used for effect, or it can catch the author out when making minor edits. If you change a sentence, read it again to make sure it still means what you want it to – this is something an editor or proofreader will not be able to do for you.

Related to structure is numbering. The number of levels that a writer goes to is an indication as to how well structured the information is. As a rule of thumb aim to structure information so that only three, or at most, four levels of numbering are used. This book has been written so that only three levels are required, for example 1.2.3.

Note. Avoid cross-references where possible, they make any document difficult to use. It is often better to summarize the key points and put the reference in brackets rather than baldly refer the reader elsewhere. They may not come back.

Fact, feature and benefit

Presenting information can be done in many ways; a telephone directory is chock full of facts, but if you want to get someone to phone you, then they need a reason for doing so.

Here is the exactly the same information presented in three different ways:

1 The plain facts	The car has air conditioning.
2 With added features	The car has air conditioning that can cope with a wide range of outside temperatures.
3 What is in it for you?	The ability to keep the temperature low even when the outside temperature is high will significantly improve the comfort of Mr Rebecki who lives in a subtropical part of Australia.

This may be a trivial example, but it is clear which one is likely to be the more persuasive to this potential car buyer.

Presenting information is most important in the specialist and technical sections of a bid document. This is in part because the writers tend to take it as read; because they know what the benefits are they do not see the need to point it out. Another, perhaps more relevant example:

Original version	The XYZ server uses state-of-the art technology that includes 'hot-swappable' disk drives.
Improved version	The XYZ server that is proposed for NB's application supports disk drives that can be 'hot swapped'[*fact*]. This means that in the event of a failure the system can keep running while the failed component is replaced with a new one [*feature*]. Consequently NB will be able to deliver their on-line hotel room booking service on a 365 days a year basis, minimizing any chance of lost revenue due to equipment failure [*benefit*].

This is still fairly technical language, but it is clear that the client will benefit from the choice of equipment in a way that is directly relevant to their business.

Key point. Benefits are only valid if they are directly relevant to the audience. If the car buyer had lived in a more temperate climate and was on a fixed, modest, retirement income, then fuel economy might have been more useful than air conditioning. Know your audience.

Writing styles

Everybody has their own style of writing. It is a bit like the way a person walks or speaks. Although it is hard to change the fundamental approach someone has to writing it is relatively easy to look at certain aspects and make significant improvements. Areas worth addressing include positive language, use of the active rather than the passive voice, consistency of approach, vocabulary, care in the use of cliché and slang, and keeping things short and to the point.

POSITIVE VS NEGATIVE

When writing a bid, it should always be in the back of the mind that the intention is to persuade the reader to accept your proposition. Consequently, anything written for a bid should be put in positive terms. Any question posed should lead to a 'yes' answer rather than a 'no'. For example, if the bidding organization has never worked with a particular client before, but has worked in the same market sector, then this information could be expressed as:

Negative/neutral	Although BS has not worked with NB before it has considerable experience within the industry.
Positive	BS will bring its considerable experience from working within the industry to allow NB to deliver its services more efficiently than its competitors.

Neither of the above is bad, but the second example gives a much more positive impression to the reader.

ACTIVE VS PASSIVE

First, what does this mean? In technical grammatical terms the definition of the active voice is one in which the subject of the verb performs the action described by the verb. Similarly, the passive voice is defined as being when the subject is the recipient of the action of the verb. If this does not make it any clearer the following examples will.

Active	BS plc won the government's export achievement award.
Passive	BS plc have been selected by the government to win an export achievement award.

In both cases the information is the same, but it is the active voice that conveys the more positive image. So, now that the difference between active and passive voice is understood, which is better for use in a bid document? In general it is better to use the active voice as it is simpler to understand and is more dynamic to read.

CONSISTENCY

Whatever style is adopted for writing a particular section of a bid document it will read better if it is consistent. It can be disconcerting to have an abrupt change mid-paragraph. Take the following example:

NB Ltd has been selected by many companies to provide telephone and telecommunications services. It has considerable expertise and represents a safe choice. Many government departments including the Ministry of Misinformation (MoM) are current users of NB's services and equipment. You are going to be knocked out by the way we put our products into your business. We really make telecommunications hum.

An extreme case perhaps and it is hard to imagine anyone using the language and style of the final two sentences in a bid to a government agency.

Consistency also applies to the way information is presented. It is easier for the reader if lists are always given in the same way, and use of bullet points, numbering, labelling of figures and so forth are consistent from start to finish.

VOCABULARY

There is a temptation to use words when writing that you would not use when speaking. This needs to be watched, as there are two pitfalls here. The first is that you may use the word incorrectly and appear ignorant or clumsy. The second is that you may sound pretentious. This does not mean you should ignore your vocabulary but you should temper any desire to impress with the needs of the audience and the need to write a bid document that is easy to read.

> *Note*. Estimates vary, but it is thought that an educated person will have a vocabulary of about 15 000 words. Some people know more than 25 000! However, in everyday use most people will use up to about 2000 of them. So it makes sense to keep to the familiar if the aim is ease of use.

CLICHÉ AND SLANG

Using clichés is something that needs to be done with care. Some clichés are simply awful, for example 'at this moment in time' – just use 'now'. Others allow the writer to say something with a short phrase that would otherwise have to be said using a great many words. 'Tried and tested' implies far more than you could easily capture in as few words trying to get across the same concept. Do not use a cliché unless you are sure that the readers will be familiar with it and will understand it in the same way that the writer does.

There are also 'business-speak' clichés that seem to crop up with monotonous regularity in bids and proposals. One of these reads something like this: 'NB is pleased to have the opportunity to respond to this invitation to tender.' There are others and they are most often found in the management summary and in covering letters. Use them with caution, particularly when bidding to a client for the second time. They will have read it before and it will lack even more credibility.

Related to this use of cliché is the use of slang. It is never acceptable to use foul language in a bid document and it is assumed that nobody reading this book would even dream of doing so. However, there are many words in common usage that have a meaning that may not be found in a dictionary, or have become changed over time. Others stem from youth culture, for example the word 'cool' became an indication of approval and many people still use it in conversation. It would not be appropriate to use it in a bid, or any other formal business document.

LESS IS MORE

A cliché no less! A common problem for the inexperienced writer is using 10 words when three will do. As mentioned earlier, 'at this moment in time' is more succinctly put as 'now'. There are non-cliché examples of this too. 'Take into consideration' becomes 'consider'. 'In the event of' becomes 'if'.

Similarly, it is worth looking at the actual words used to see if a shorter one might be more effective. 'Terminate' can be replaced by 'end', 'commence' by 'start' and so forth. The author commonly commits this sin by using 'however' instead of 'but'. Changing to a shorter word should not be done at the risk of changing the emphasis of what was meant. English is notorious for having large numbers of choices for a given word. Have a look in a copy of a thesaurus for examples. However, the choices given do not always have exactly the same meaning. For example, an alternative given in a thesaurus used by the author for 'detail' is 'aspect'. These are not always interchangeable.

Another way to save words is to avoid the needless negative. Rather than say, 'it is not uncommon' say 'it is common' or 'commonly'. This is the old joke of, 'never, never, use a double negative!' People get into the habit of doing this in conversation because it buys them thinking time. This is one case where you should not try to write in the same way that you talk.

Allied to this is sentence length, covered in more detail in Chapter 8 on editing. You should aim for sentences that vary between 10 and 20 words – give or take a few. Having several very short sentences becomes irritating, for example: 'NB makes soap powder. It is a market leader. It has been in business for ten years.' On the other hand, long complicated sentences can be confusing. Consider this: 'NB was established in 1984 and has a number of brands in the crowded soap market sector, which is estimated at in excess of three billion zogs per year; NB owns over thirty five per cent of this market at the time of writing and can thus call itself the market leader, having ten per cent more than the nearest competitor.' It is easy to see that somewhere in between these extremes is what should be aimed for.

> Hint. A good way to check on the style of any written passage is to read it out loud. If it sounds stilted, disjointed or in any way odd, consider rewriting it.

Finally, along the lines of less is more, using a diagram, a chart or a picture not only saves thousands of words but also breaks up the text and makes the document look better (see Chapter 9 on layout and presentation for more suggestions relating to appearance).

Writing a (management) summary

There is a school of thought that maintains that you cannot write the management summary before the rest of the bid is completed. This is not always true. It also means that by leaving the management summary until last you guarantee that there will not be enough time left to write it! In part this relates to how the bid is managed. If the bid brief method (see Part 1) is followed and you build the proposal based on clearly identified themes then it will be possible to write effective management summaries at any stage during the bid. They will change with the bid, but they will evolve with it. In some ways this debate comes down to do you design the bricks first or the house? In most bids it is a mixture of the two – what starts out as the sales strategy evolves as the detailed understanding of the client's needs changes. Also, what the client wants at the start of a bid is seldom what they want by the end of it. Change is the only constant.

It does not actually matter if you write it early or late, the technique for writing the management summary remains the same.

Step 1   Identify the key sales themes that need to be brought out. If these were identified at the start of the bid check they are the ones that have actually ended up in the body of the bid.
Step   Identify key benefits that are relevant to the client. If they are not closely related to the themes, re-examine them. Prioritize them in the order you think they matter to the client.
Step 3   Present them in a logical sequence, ideally with a link from one to the next.
Step 4   Have an introductory paragraph that describes the points that you are about to raise and why they are relevant to the client.
Step 5   Make sure no new information has been included that is not supported in the rest of the bid.
Step 6   Sum up the benefits in a final paragraph that ends on a high.
Step 7   Get someone else to read it and tell you what they think it says.

Note: this method actually works for writing any summary.

Annexes and appendices

There will inevitably be information in a bid document that is complex or only partly relevant to the bid. This is the prompt to use annexes/appendices. The former are stand-alone, separate documents. The latter are supplements to existing documents. When to use these is a judgement call. It is undesirable to have unreadable legal/technically complex material in the middle of a bid as it breaks up the flow and takes the focus off the selling argument. It is also undesirable to have information that is only partially relevant to the bid, such as last year's accounts, as well. Where such information is needed then an annex is the place to put it.

> *Note*. There is a temptation to throw into an annex anything that might be vaguely useful, 'Just in case'. Try and resist this. If you cannot think of a reason why the information is beneficial to the reader, leave it out.

Plain English

It is very easy to get carried away when writing. Many people who speak clearly and simply suddenly get the urge to use complex words that they would not use in conversation. They will also start to produce complicated and confusing sentences that would require the lungs of an ox to say out loud. This is a shame as the result is often very uncomfortable to read. The late Enoch Powell used to maintain that if you could not translate a sentence easily into

Latin then it was probably poor when it was in English. Not everyone has his facility for ancient languages, but the concept can be translated into the reading aloud test. If in doubt about any paragraph or sentence just read it aloud and see if it works and means what you thought it did when it was written.

Note. The Plain English society offers some very useful guidelines on writing, which the author recommends even if he does not always follow them! (*The Plain English Guide*, ISBN 0-19-860049, Oxford University Press)

Covering letter

Whenever anything is submitted to the client there is an opportunity to include a covering letter. Take this opportunity, not only does it look professional and polite, but it also gives you the chance to make a point, or ask a question. This can be useful for making your own organization look better than the competition, or raising an issue which will make them question the competency of the opposition. For example, you may have established that none of the competitors have ever traded with the client before. It might be worth mentioning how long you have had a business relationship with them to sow a seed of doubt about the devil that they do not know.

Note. This sort of thing needs to be done with finesse. Never let it seem that you are knocking the other bidders, it will rebound upon you.

When you come to write a covering letter, irrespective of any points you may wish to score, there are some basics that need to be included. These may seem obvious, but it is surprising how many times something gets missed. It is not unknown in the world of procurement for information to arrive from a bidder without any identification as who sent it, and what it was for!

Proofreading

When it comes to documents that are going to be seen by a client, no amount of proofreading is too much. Ideally this should be done by someone other than the writer, as it is hard to spot mistakes if you already know what is coming next. If there is an editor associated with the bid team then that person may be available to proofread as part of the job. Even if this is the case, or someone else is available, the writer should still make a practice of making a first pass at proofreading to eliminate the more obvious errors. For the writer proofreading should cover the spelling, the grammar and checking the arithmetic in, for example, pricing.

When proofreading do not set impossible goals; it will not be possible to eliminate every error. Indeed, the introduction of spelling and grammar checkers in most word processing and desktop publishing systems means that the errors that are there are often very hard to detect.

CASE STUDY

SITUATION

BS plc were asked to bid for the provision of a traffic control system that included traffic signals, control room equipment, telecommunications and computer equipment, and closed circuit television cameras and monitors. They were not required to install, maintain or operate this equipment, so the bid was turned over to the equipment manufacturing arm of the company. The operational group handled most bids for BS plc. Consequently, this part of the company did not often get directly involved in bids as it normally only answered the technical specification questions that were passed on from the operational arm of the organization.

PROBLEM

The staff writing the bid had excellent technical skills and understood the equipment requirement very well. They were able to put together a first-rate portfolio of equipment that would meet all the requirements of the client. In addition, because the equipment chosen met but did not exceed these requirements, the price was a good one. A good price and solution ought to give a good chance of winning the bid. However, the writing skills of these people was more suited to producing technical specifications than to selling the virtues of the equipment. The equipment and the requirement were well understood and the copy that was written detailed the functions and specifications of the equipment comprehensively. Unfortunately, it did not show how the equipment would benefit the client. For example, the flexibility of some of the control equipment was such that one unit could be used for many functions which would allow commonality of spares and the ability to swap units to keep the system running in cases of breakdowns. This would have been a significant benefit to the client who would

have been able to reduce spares holding, thus saving money. Furthermore the reliability of the system would have been high, significantly reducing the chances of traffic chaos due to failures. Neither of these benefits was made clear in the bid. It was assumed that the readers would understand this and work it out for themselves. On top of this much of the bid was written in highly technical language, with no summaries to explain the basics for the benefit of the non-technical bid evaluators.

OUTCOME

The bid as delivered had a good price associated with it and actually had a very good solution for the client's requirements. Sadly, it was all written in highly technical and somewhat obscure jargon. This was bad enough, but none of it related to how it would solve the client's problem, nor did it make clear how the client's business would benefit from using NB's products. Consequently, BS were hard put to decide if this was good or bad. They were pushed for time. They had to get the new equipment in place within weeks, so they did not have time to go back to NB to ask questions. NB lost the sale to a competitor that had a more expensive offering but that had made it clear that they could do the job and that BS would benefit very quickly from taking their offering.

LESSON LEARNT

NB decided to send their technical staff on both a 'Plain English' and a sales writing course. They wanted to make sure that future bids they contributed to were understandable and demonstrated clear, relevant, benefits to the client. They also wanted to reduce the time that the people who usually produced bids had been spending in taking the raw technical information and turning it into selling copy. Consequently, they were able to respond to clients more quickly. In addition the technical support staff gained increased job satisfaction from becoming more involved in the sales process instead of being treated as human technical specifications.

Checklist

Item	Description	Completed?
The basics	Is the spelling correct (and is it the right word, e.g. 'to' vs. 'too')? Is the grammar correct? Is there a summary at the start? Do you need a conclusion at the end? If so, do not put any new information in it. Are there any analogies that are likely to confuse the reader? Is all the information relevant to the reader and the subject? Can you usefully shorten any of the longer sentences?	
Writing style	Have you taken into account: Active/passive voice? Vocabulary? Positive/negative language? Is what you have written consistent?	
Plain English	Is it easy to read and understand? Can it be made easier?	
Questions	Have you answered the questions asked?	
Benefits	Have you related facts and features to benefits to the client?	
Audience	Do you know who you are writing for? Have you taken this into account?	

8 *Editorial Skills*

Everyone needs an editor. (Tim Foote, in an article concerning the fact that Hitler's *Mein Kampf* was originally titled *Four and a Half Years of Struggle against Lies, Stupidity and Cowardice*)

In any bid that involves more than one person there will inevitably be a stage when their contributions have to merge into one document. At this point there will be a need for an editor. This will be a thankless task because everyone thinks that their written work is perfect and any attempt to change it will be resented. However, editing is an essential task, as without it the delivered document will be fragmented, inconsistent and look a mess. Because it is a thankless task, and because it will be the Bid Manager's responsibility to deliver the bid, this job will often end up with the Bid Manager. The other person it can end up with is the person supporting the bid as an administrator. If you can get a professional editor or technical author with sales experience to do this job for you, and the budget or the size of the bid justifies it, then do so. If not, then this chapter gives the layman's guide to editing a bid (Figure 8.1).

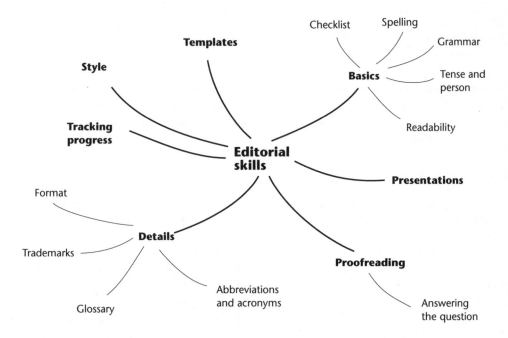

Figure 8.1 *Mind Map®: Editorial skills*

Note. The role of the editor has been liberally interpreted here; anyone who is familiar with the role of the editor in a publishing environment will have a somewhat different view. No mention is given to proofing marks as it is assumed that the editor will do the work on line. This is what happens in a bid environment.

The basics

The most important ground rule for anyone undertaking, or having thrust upon them, the role of editor is to have a clear definition of what is to be delivered. The role of the editor is most definitely *not* to write the bits of any bid document that have been forgotten or not delivered by sales or senior management. Identification of what is missing, ensuring that the documents meet style guidelines, spell checking and getting it ready for production are the roles of the editor. If you are the editor make sure that the role is clearly defined before you start.

SPELLING

Getting the spelling right is the first duty of the editor. This is made easier by the provision of spell checkers in the majority of word processing packages. However, there can be snags with these if they are not geared up to the version of English in use in your country. Many default to the United States' version of English which, for example, spells colour incorrectly (if you are British) as color. You need to obtain the correct dictionary for your document and set up the word processing application to use it.

It should be noted that the dictionaries provided as standard may have some eccentricities. For example the one used by the author does not recognize the word consultancy, hardly an uncommon word. The solution to this was to add it to the custom dictionary that was supplied with the application.

Use of a spell checker will quickly cure 95 per cent or more of the spelling errors. However, there will also be errors that they do not detect, such as use of the wrong word. For example, 'form' instead of 'from' is a common mistake. You need to read documents to see if they make sense to detect this kind of thing. Again, this is where it can be very difficult to proofread your own document.

GRAMMAR

As with spell checking there are grammar checkers provided with word processing applications. Be warned, these are often of dubious value. However, they can be helpful in detecting where a correctly spelt but wrong word has crept into a sentence. If grammar checkers are available it is worth trying them out to see if they are more help or hindrance. If you are in doubt about grammatical points *The Plain English Guide*, (Oxford University Press) or *Fowler's Modern English Usage* (Clarendon Press) will help. Keep in mind that this is a bid and do not get too bogged down in grammatical exactitude. For example, it is not that important if the items in a list start with capital letters and end with full stops or small letters and commas, as long as you are consistent and it is clear what is meant.

> *Note.* Know your audience. If you are writing for an individual or a profession that is grammatically picky then get it right. The author has had bad experiences with ex-schoolteachers in this respect.

There are some basic mistakes that come up time and time again in every bid or, to be honest, most business writing. It can be worth issuing these as a checklist to those involved in writing for the bid. Even if they do not follow them they will not be able to hold it against the editor when their precious words are changed. What follows should be taken more as a checklist than a serious attempt by a semi-literate author to provide a course in English grammar:

Singular and plural	Limited companies (and plcs) are singular. 'BS Ltd is a leading supplier of XYZ.' Do not say, 'BS Ltd are a leading supplier.' This is most often done in a follow-on sentence where the company becomes 'we'. For example, 'BS Ltd is a leading supplier of XYZ with many years experience. *We* are familiar with the MNO market … '.
	Another issue with plurals relates to which word should be made plural in a sentence. The classic, but usually unhelpful example refers to courts martial as the plural of court martial, the courts being plural, not the type of court. If in any doubt simply ask what is it that is plural, it is usually obvious.
	Finally, make sure that the verb and the noun agree. They should either both be singular or both plural. For example: 'The *Prime Minister* is out of the country. The spin *doctors* are on holiday.'
Possessives, apostrophes (and plurals again)	When to put in the apostrophe is always fun. The basic rule is that 's is added to a word to indicate something that belongs. For example, 'The cat's whiskers' refers to the whiskers belonging to a particular cat. 'The cats' whiskers' refers to the whiskers on a whole bunch of cats. This gets messy where words end in s in the first place. Then the apostrophe goes after the word, dropping off the extra 's', for example, The Loch Ness' Monster.
	Something that is surprisingly common, but gives the impression that the writer is totally illiterate, is missing out the apostrophe in condensed words. For example 'cant' instead of 'can't', 'wont' instead of 'won't'. Spell checkers will not pick up all of these (cant and wont are perfectly good words), indeed they are often responsible for causing them in the first place.
	It's and its are commonly confused too. This is partly because it seems to contradict the normal possessive rule described above. 'Its' is an adjective meaning belonging to, for example: 'The paint has lost its gloss.' 'It's' is an abbreviation of 'it is'. 'It's not fair' expands to 'It is not fair'.
	A classic error of this kind crops up time and again in the IT world. People apply a spell checker to the abbreviation PC (personal computer) and end up with PC's (belonging to the PC) when they actually meant a number of PCs (plural).
Lists	The correct way to punctuate a sentence that contains a list is to follow a colon (:) with items starting with a small letter followed by a semi-colon (;) until the last item which is followed with a full stop. For example:

What follows is a list:
first item;
second item;
last item.

However, some grammar checkers disagree with this. Also, it is the author's view that this gets us into the 'picky' territory. For most purposes it is perfectly acceptable to use any reasonable alternative, but be consistent within a document. For example, the following may not be perfect English but it is clear:

What follows is a list –
First,
Second,
Third.

LONG SENTENCES

It is very easy for people writing bids to get carried away and write very long sentences that are almost like streams of consciousness. These need to be broken up, particularly where any of the readers are likely to be non-native English speakers. The author acknowledges that this is one of his own faults. It is worth remembering the journalist's motto, 'make it short, make it snappy, make it up'. Take the following example:

Long sentence	Shorter, better, punchy sentence
A key benefit of the BS solution is that it allows NB Ltd to reduce the time it takes to sign up a new customer to its property management service to two hours thus enabling them to gain 24-hour and maintenance provision paid for through a single monthly payment.	Adopting the BS solution will provide NB with the ability to sign up customers to its property service in under two hours. These customers will then benefit from: • 24-hour security; • 24-hour maintenance; • single monthly payments.

The sentence has been shortened and the benefits have been broken out as a series of bullet points. This makes them more obvious to the reader.

Another way to shorten sentences is to look for phrases that can be replaced with a single word. For example, 'in a very few instances' can become 'seldom'. These are usually many opportunities to do this because of phrases that have passed from spoken to written language that were created solely with the point of buying time. For example, people say, 'at this moment in time' instead of 'now'. It is worth questioning the usefulness of phrases such as, 'taking these points into consideration'. What actual value are they adding?

There is also scope for cutting down the word count by turning unnecessary negatives into simple positives. 'We are not averse to negotiations on this point' becomes 'We are happy to negotiate this' or even 'This is negotiable'.

> *Note.* Do not get too carried away with shortening sentences. It is not a Holy Grail. In fact if you split everything down into staccato fragments it becomes irritating to read. Longer sentences help the flow of a passage and make it pleasant, and easy, to read.

PERSON

Agree with the bid team what the person is going to be before anyone starts writing. The author's recommendation for the majority of bids is to use the third person. For example, do not say, 'You will recognize the benefits of the proposed solution', or 'We expect that BS plc will welcome our approach ...'. Keep it more formal, 'BS Ltd will recognize the benefits of the proposed solution', or 'NB Ltd expect that BS plc will welcome our approach ... '.

Whatever standard you do choose, apply it to the whole document, or at least to an entire major section if it was decided to adopt a different style for different readers.

READABILITY CHECK

There are many readability checkers available and many word processing systems now have them built in. These will typically use some combination of sentence length, characters per word and the complexity of the sentence structure. For those who do not have access to one of these checkers the following is offered as a simple guide. You can use this for an individual paragraph, a page, a section or an entire document. Most of the time it will be most helpful with a troublesome paragraph or section (which needs to be at least 100 words long). Analysing an entire document will be very time consuming.

Step 1   Count the number of words in the text under review (W_{total}). Count the number of sentences (S_{total}). Divide W_{total} by S_{total} to get W_{ps}.

Step 2   Count the number of words with three or more syllables per 100 words. Ignore composite words such as bookkeeper, hyphenated words such as event-horizon, capitalized words and three syllable words ending in 'es' or 'ed' that are verbs (such as demotes). This gives the number N_{ts}.

Step 3   The readability index (RI) is obtained by adding together the numbers from steps 1 and 2 and multiplying the result by 0.4. $RI = 0.4(W_{ps} + N_{ts})$

This should give you a number somewhere between 6 and 20. If not, check the calculation or make sure you have a realistic sample of text.

RI	Comments
< 10	What you have is easy to read and most adults will have no trouble reading and understanding it, even if English is not their first language.
10 to 12	This is still easy to read for anyone whose first language is English, but some non-native speakers may start to struggle.
12 to 16	This is getting more difficult. The writer is now making assumptions about the education and grasp of English of the reader. It may be worth spending time reviewing this material to simplify it. In most cases it will be an easy matter of shortening sentences.
> 16	At this level the audience needs to be well educated and a native English speaker. This may be acceptable for specialist passages aimed at a specialist audience but the management summary certainly should not read this way.

This book has been aimed mainly at people with English as their first language working in a professional environment. Most passages have an RI of between 10 and 14. The style is suitable for most proposals but could certainly be made easier for different audiences. The author is aiming to enjoy himself as well as communicate.

For those looking for a guide to using English effectively then *The Plain English Guide* (Oxford University Press) is strongly recommended. Anyone performing the role of editor will find this a helpful reference work.

Note. Detailed technical information may be difficult to make readable. This also may apply to contract schedules and the like. Suggest to the writer that this material may be better placed in an annex to the main bid.

CHECKLIST

In Chapter 7 there was a 'get you started' checklist for writers. This checklist makes sense for editors too, but with additions relating to consistency and proofreading:

Item	Completed?
Is the spelling correct (and is it the right word, e.g. 'to' vs. 'too')?	
Is the grammar correct?	
Is there a summary at the start?	
Is a conclusion needed at the end? If so, make sure no new information has been put in it.	
Are there any analogies that are likely to confuse the reader?	
Is all the information relevant to the reader and the subject?	
Can long sentences be usefully broken up into shorter ones?	
Is information presented in the best way?	
Are heading styles consistent?	
Are all the pages numbered, dated and copyrighted?	
Are acronyms and abbreviations used consistently?	

Templates

If the organization that the editor is working for does not already have standards for the documents it releases into the outside world then it is a good idea to invent them. If they do exist, use them. If needed, Chapter 9 gives some pointers to designing bid documents and presentation material. However, time spent setting up basic templates for both authors and the editor early on in the bid process will be an excellent investment.

It is also worth considering setting up a bid document skeleton. This document has all the styles, type fonts, numbering systems and so forth defined and has all the top-level headings already in place. Many government procurements will specify this structure anyway, so you may not even have to think it up in the first place. The more that can be done at the start to get the basics in place, the less time will be wasted at the end when the pressure will be on.

Some words of caution about using templates. In most word processing systems it is possible to set up a template document that defines text, heading styles and the like that can then be issued to the contributors to the bid. Sadly, these templates are not set in cement and the authors can easily, often accidentally, overwrite the template formatting.

> *Note.* The main theme of this book is the apparent lack of time available when producing a bid. Editorial work is a good example of where work invested at the beginning of the bid can make a significant reduction in the work needed at the end of the bid.

Tracking changes

It is usually the responsibility of the Bid Manager to get the various contributions to the bid in on time. Whoever does this, the contributions will not all arrive on schedule or in the order that is easiest for the editor. To keep track of things the editor should keep a progress chart based upon the bid structure. An example of part of such a chart is given here:

Section	Author draft due/actual	Edited	Reviewed by author	Issued
1 Introduction	23/05/06– 24/05/06	25/05/6	26/05/06	
2 Requirement	30/05/06			
2.1 Requirement Summary	25/05/06			
2.2 Building requirement	28/05/06			

It can be helpful to print out a large version of this chart and keep it on the wall, filling in the boxes as each element is completed, using a highlighter pen. This provides a very visual indication of what is missing and what remains to be done.

Another issue relating to collating information is spotting gaps. Again the chart will make it clear if there any gaps.

> *Hint.* If you are going to get contributions from people using wildly different word processing and desktop publishing systems, then consider asking them to supply their words as plain text (ASCII) with no formatting. You can then cut and paste this text into the document template, or bid skeleton, without the risk of messing up the carefully set up styles.

Style(s)

First the editor needs to ensure the 'mechanical' elements are consistent. Get the basics right as described earlier before worrying about anything more sophisticated. If time is at a premium make the basics the priority. Then consider looking at the writing style.

There are many elements that go to make up writing style and they are specific to the writer. Factors include, vocabulary used, length of sentences, use of passive and active voice, positive and negative language (see Chapter 7 for guidance on active and passive voice and positive and negative language). It is not recommended that the person editing a bid try to change the writer's style, as there simply will not be time to do it. If the editor feels that there is room for improvement then go back to the writer and make positive suggestions, give examples for the next draft and do try to be diplomatic.

Where time permits, the editor should try to get some consistency of writing style throughout any delivered bid document. However, different audiences need written information provided in different styles if they are to be comfortable with reading it. This can be an issue if the editor does not understand every audience. In reality the editor is unlikely to have this desirable skill. Consequently, where the editor does not know the intended audience well it is necessary to restrict such editorial activity to the minimum. The editor will not have time to rewrite the entire bid.

> *Key point.* Once something has been edited it is essential to get the original author to reread it and agree that it still means what it did when he or she wrote it, at least in terms of points of fact.

The details

Attention to detail is an excellent quality in an editor; if nothing else it comes in useful when sorting out such things as abbreviations, acronyms, trademarks, logos and so on. This section covers these details.

ABBREVIATIONS AND ACRONYMS

Bitter experience has shown that, no matter how well an editor or Bid Manager defines rules for abbreviations, acronyms and so forth, many people will still do their own thing. One strategy is to correct the first draft of each person's documents then send it back to them for further work asking them not to change acronyms and abbreviations. This helps – 90 per cent of the time they will not get changed.

At the same time compile all the acronyms and abbreviations into an electronic file so that they can be used for easy reference or given to authors as a starting point. If this file is kept in alphabetical order then it will provide a useful glossary that may be included with the bid.

If you are using a word processing package or a desktop publishing system that supports macros then it may be possible to automate the process of making these elements consistent. The time to do this is when you create the register of abbreviations and acronyms. For every entry you can either write a macro to find alternatives and replace them, or you can add the correct versions to a spell-checking dictionary. Time spent during the earlier, 'quieter' times of a bid can save considerable effort later during production frenzies. Indeed, acronyms and abbreviations are often the things that get left out during last minute panics because they lose out during the 'what's important vs time available' argument.

It may be possible to add acronyms and abbreviations to the dictionary used by the spell checker in your word processing application. This can save time as it means that the abbreviations will get sorted out at the same time as the spell check.

Even if a glossary including all the acronyms and abbreviations is included within a bid document, the golden rule is to expand it the first time it is used in a stand-alone part of a document. For example: 'The current weather at an airport is obtained from a Meteorological Airfield Report (METAR). You can get a METAR on the Internet.'

LOGOS, COMPANY NAMES AND TRADEMARKS

As with acronyms and abbreviations, the task here is to keep them consistent and, in addition, make sure they have been used in accordance with any restrictions imposed by their owners where possible. With trademarks it usually sufficient just to recognize them, for example Microsoft Excel™. However, be careful to make sure they are reproduced accurately. Check that the same version of each logo has been used throughout the bid documents. If more than one version is encountered, choose the one that permission has been gained for. Make sure that logos print well in colour, black and white and grey scale. This is important if the document is to be printed on monochrome as well as on colour printers. It also matters for photocopying, you want the document to be easy to reproduce for the client.

It is helpful to maintain an electronic file with copies of all the trademarks, logos and company names, as they are to appear in the bid. This can be distributed to authors for reference, and saves time wasted in having to look them up each time.

> *Note.* Do not aim for anything more than consistency within the bid documents. One customer of the author's never managed to have consistent rules for how their name should be presented. Some standards specified upper case, some specified capital letter followed by lower case, some specified bold type and so on. All these standards were current and approved – all were contradictory.

GLOSSARY

Having created a list of abbreviations and acronyms, company and trade names and so on to help with the editorial task, the editor is in possession of a glossary. Some enlightened procurement organizations ask for a glossary in order to make reading complex technical bids easier for those evaluating them. Where they do not it can only benefit the bidder to include one. This is a spin-off benefit from doing the editorial spadework. Do have a glossary if time permits.

FORMAT

Whilst not normally a task associated with being an editor, in the bid environment someone has to make sure that all the pages have the right format, that the layout meets the requirements chosen for the bid. It will typically end up with whoever undertakes the editorial role. This will be a mechanical exercise that can either be left until the end, if a mad panic is desired, or worked on as the bid progresses. Using templates as discussed before can be a big help here. There are no short cuts; every page needs to be checked to make sure that it conforms to the layout required.

Proofreading

Proofreading is very important. Lack of time should be the only factor which reduces the amount of proofreading done. Unfortunately it is very hard for people to proofread their own material. This is largely because the writer knows what is coming next so will be unlikely to pick up on missing words and so forth. So somebody else needs to do it. Sadly, much of this will end up with the person who owns the role of editor. Judicious use of spell checkers, templates and other automated tools will help reduce this, at least for the mechanical aspects such as spelling and some grammar. However, it is still necessary to check that the correct word is used and to make sure that page breaks and numbering all make sense, and so forth.

In general it is easier to pick up errors in a hard copy than it is on screen, though obviously it is easier to edit on line (making sure you always have a back-up copy of the original to go back to). The hard copy version will make it much easier to spot problems with page breaks and layout issues that may look just fine on the screen. Make sure that the printer used for proofing is the same one that will be used for the actual production run. Different printers can produce different results from the same electronic document, sometimes even if they are the same model and make!

Hint. If there is an independent team (for example a Red team) whose role is to review the bid, ask them to note any proofing points they pick up on their individual copy. The more eyes the better.

ANSWERING THE QUESTION

In the chapter on writing skills much was made of the importance of answering the question put by the client, not one that the writer would like to have been asked. Along with the mechanical aspects of proofreading, the author should check to see that questions have been answered. Of course, it may be beyond the editor's technical skill to know if the answer is correct or even on the right lines. However, if it is not clear to the editor that there is a response to each question that provides the answer, then it will not be clear to an evaluator.

A common example is the multiple part question. The client may have made a general request for information and then followed it up with a number of sub-questions relating to particular details. It is very easy in the heat of a bid for the writer responsible for answering the question to answer the main part and then miss out one of the supplementary points. The editor should check for this as part of the proofreading exercise.

Presentations

Most of what has been written in this chapter relates to proposals and other bid documents. However, an editorial role can also be of benefit when producing presentations and the supporting material that goes with them. The areas where editorial support can help include the following:

Slides	Spelling
	Type fonts and text styles
	Grammar
	Use of logos, abbreviations and acronyms
	Layout and design
	Structure and readability
Handouts	As above plus page breaks, editorial review of accompanying notes and consistency with house styles.

In addition, the editor can make sure that where there are to be several presenters their presentations link together seamlessly. As with bid documents it is worth looking at the slides and handouts in their printed form as well as on screen. This will minimize the chances of any surprises during the production stage.

CASE STUDY

SITUATION

BS Ltd had to submit a proposal for the supply of security equipment to NB plc, a group that operated office and warehouse facilities. In addition to the equipment itself, mainly surveillance cameras, the proposal had to cover installation, relocation, maintenance and consultancy on the appropriate type and location of equipment for any specified building. BS had two separate departments that supplied equipment and offered operational consultancy. The maintenance and installation services it provided via a subcontractor. The sales manager, Jimmy C, split the requirements document that came from NB into the three parts that related to these areas and passed them on to the relevant departments and the subcontractor. Jimmy intended to collate the three documents together, write a management summary, and build a price based upon the quotes from the departments/subcontractor.

PROBLEM

When the individual sections came back to Jimmy it became horribly clear that they were not going to dovetail smoothly together. To start with each had used a different type font, size and margin settings. They had also used different headers and footers, numbering and heading styles. Visually the documents looked very different. There were also huge differences in writing styles. The subcontractor had taken a very friendly approach and had used you and we all over the place, and had adopted an eccentric numbering system. The two departmental contributions were more alike, but again very different writing styles had been used. In addition, one department had two levels of numbering, the other five – what was a high-level heading in one document was a low-level one in the other.

The formatting problems for the overall page layout were not too great – Jimmy was able to cut and paste into a template document. However, the nature of the word processing system meant that he had to go through all the headings one by one to get them to the correct style. This took a considerable amount of time and there was little time to do much more than this if the pricing and management summary were to be completed.

In the end it was a matter of fixing as much as possible, writing a management summary at the last minute and hoping for the best. The only thing that looked good was the price! Jimmy hoped that this would be low enough to save the day.

OUTCOME

The delivered bid looked and read like what it was – a badly assembled patchwork quilt. Because there was so little time available for the editorial task there was not time to do much more than get some of the type fonts consistent and put the page breaks in the right places. The writing styles were completely inconsistent and, of course, did not reference each other (an additional issue was the lack of an overall sales strategy). Furthermore, each section had been numbered differently, used completely different styles for headings, captions, titles and legends and so on. Although the raw information was actually quite good, the poor presentation and inconsistencies made the client worry about quality standards within BS and they did not feel they wanted to trade with BS. Even the low price was not enough to sway them.

LESSON LEARNT

The key point was not to leave the editorial work until the last minute. The amount of work that would have been needed to do a good job on the randomly produced components of the final bid would easily have kept an entire team busy for over a week. Jimmy had one day! If document templates and writing guidelines had been produced at the beginning, perhaps with a skeleton document for the contributors to populate as a starting point, life would have been much easier for Jimmy.

Checklist

Item	Description	Completed?
The basics	Spelling Grammar Readability	
The details	Abbreviations Acronyms Logos Company names Trademarks Glossary Format	
Proofreading	Have you done enough? Are all questions answered?	
Presentations	Spelling Grammar Readability Abbreviations Acronyms Logos Company names Trademarks Links Format	

9 *Layout and Presentation*

Always design a thing by considering it in its next larger context – a chair in a room, a room in a house, a house in an environment. (Eliel Saarinen, 1956)

'If it looks right, it probably is right' is a phrase often used in the world of aircraft design. The phrase can probably be traced back rather further than that; at the very least it has roots in the concept of form and function promoted by William Morris in the nineteenth century. Getting things to look right goes back even further than that. The Ancient Greeks put their faith in the golden ratio where the ratio of the width to the length of a rectangle is the same as the ratio of the length to the length plus the width. The golden number works out at about 1.61. Out of interest the 'A' series of paper (for example A4) has a ratio of 1.6. One of the reasons that people admire Classical and Georgian architecture is because it makes use of this ratio in the proportions and placement of doors, windows and the design of façades.

Enough of the lecture, what things look like matters and this is doubly true for bid documents. However well you know your client, however strong your business relationship, if a third-rate looking document is put in then it can only harm your cause. Similarly if your

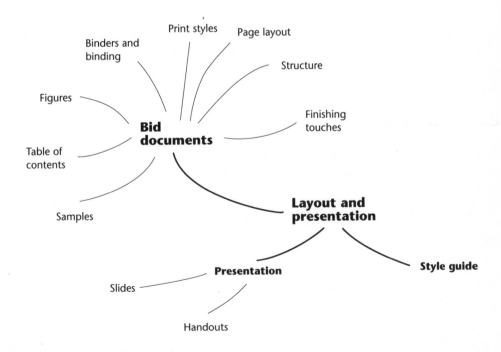

Figure 9.1 *Mind Map®: Layout and presentation*

bid is the most attractive and easy to use then it can only benefit your cause. Research has shown that a document that makes a good first impression will be scored more highly than another with identical information that makes a poor one. This is just the same for interviews, presentations and public speaking. In this chapter some practical, rule-of-thumb suggestions will be made that can be used to improve the look and feel of the finished bid documents, and some pointers will be given for slide and handout material for use in presentations (Figure 9.1).

Suggested guidelines

The following guidelines are offered as rules of thumb for those without specific design expertise. They are offered to cover typical audiences for most commercial and government procurements. If the client audience does not fit into this broad category then it is suggested that you employ the appropriate expertise. These guidelines will deliver help to deliver an attractive and easy to use bid document.

- Use a standard size of paper (for example A4 in Europe).
- Single-sided printing may waste paper but saves time and is photocopier friendly.
- Keep the design clean, it should not look complicated or messy.
- Do not use more than two typefaces on one page.
- Do not use more than three font sizes on a page.
- Do use a type face that is easy to read and print (Times Roman and Arial are commonplace).
- Obey any layout rules specified by the client (even if they contradict any of the above).

> *Note.* Some environmentally conscious organizations insist on double-sided printing; other organizations are sensitive to potential waste. Be sensitive to this. Do not forget to allow extra production time.

Bid documents

These will mainly be in the form of proposals, responses to invitation to tenders, requests for information and so on. They will be anything from a few pages to several hundred pages long, possibly in multiple volumes. They will be produced on ordinary office paper (for example A4) and produced in house.

BID STRUCTURE

Most bid documents follow a similar structure. This may be specified by the client, if not then something along these lines is typical (an expanded version of this, together with the type of material that will go in each section is given later in the chapter):

1   Introduction;
2   Management summary;

3   Understanding of requirement;

4   Proposed solution;

5   Response to requirements (for example mandatory and desirable requirements);

6   Financial proposal (prices and payment options);

7   Annexes (brochures, annual reports, technical specifications, quality certificates and so forth).

Any design that is adopted for the bid document needs to be able to cope with all these sections and their various requirements.

PAGE LAYOUT

Every page in a bid should include the following information:

- date;
- page number;
- copyright;
- organization name;
- client name;
- bid/section title.

In addition, it is reasonable to have some sort of confidentiality statement (for example 'Commercial-in-Confidence') and it may be necessary to have a security classification such as 'Restricted', 'Confidential', 'Secret', etc. You may also be able to use graphics such as company logos, subject to copyright restrictions.

The simplest way to present this information so that it does not interfere with the rest of the document is to include it in a header and footer area. This can then be kept separate from the content area giving a clean sheet to work on.

Note. There are special rules governing documents with 'secure' information in them that must be complied with – your organization will have someone who knows the rules if you do not. Make sure these are complied with as they will impact who may have access to them.

PRINT STYLES

As mentioned before, it is recommended not to use more than two fonts on a page or, ideally, within the whole document. What type fonts should be chosen? If there is a house style with defined fonts then use them. There may even be a style guide that explains what is used where. If not, it is suggested that commonly used fonts are used – this may not make a strong design statement but it will at least mean that the document has a familiar feel to the reader.

Given that no more than two different typefaces will be used on a page, this leaves a small problem. How do you make it easy for the reader to discriminate between different heading levels, notes, comments and diagram titles? This is best done by using a combination of type sizes and attributes such as bold or italic to emphasize different functions.

For example, Figure 9.2 has been found to work well on A4-sized paper. All the main body text is in the same font, only two typefaces have been used and a combination of font size, bold and italic show the differences in function.

Style	Example
Normal text	Times New Roman 11 point
Title	**Arial 20 Point Bold (Change to suit cover page)**
Top-level heading	**Arial 14 Bold**
Second-level heading	**Times Roman 11 Bold**
Third-level heading	Arial 12
Client questions	*10 point italic*
Figure titles	*11 point italic*

Figure 9.2   *Recommended fonts*

Another question relates to type alignment, the technical term for how the left and right edges of the type line up. Some books are set using what is known as ragged right. That is the left-hand edge is straight and the right-hand edge varies according to the length of the words in relation to the right-hand margin. For most bid documents it is recommended that this style be adopted for all paragraphs. If a very formal look is required then it may be reasonable to consider what is known as 'justified text' where both left- and right-hand edges are straight lines. This can lead to some odd word spacing or overuse of hyphenation (where words are artificially split over a line break to make type fit the available space). This can be harder to read, particularly if you have non-English mother-tongue readers. It might be worth considering centred type to go underneath diagrams and figures, that is the text is centred beneath the illustration.

CHARTS, DIAGRAMS AND ILLUSTRATIONS

Although much of Part 2 refers to writing styles, it is hoped that most bid documents will contain a large amount of charts and diagrams. Pictures are not just 'worth a thousand words', but they add to the visual appeal of the document and break up potentially dull slabs of text. It should go without saying by now that any charts and diagrams used should be directly relevant to your audience, the people reading the bid. There should be a good reason for including a diagram, chart or illustration and the layout should take this into account in terms of size and prominence.

Headings

Every chart needs to have a heading associated with it that identifies it uniquely within the bid. The heading should clearly state what that chart is about. Ideally the chart should also be numbered.

Numbering

There are many ways of going about this. Some people choose to number figures according to the section/paragraph they appear in, for example, 'Figure 9.1 Sample Chart Layout'. Where more than one figure appears associated with the same paragraph then subsequent figures are given a suffix letter, 'a, b, c' and so on. Use of the word 'figure' is optional, '9.1 Sample Chart Layout' is just as clear. Others choose to number all the figures in a document sequentially, '1, 2, 3' throughout the entire document. This can then become the basis for a separate list of figures. It is the author's opinion that there is little benefit in this – figures can be incorporated in a table of contents easily with most word processing applications. So it is better to number in accordance with the part of the document the figure appears in.

> *Practical point.* If figures/diagrams are numbered sequentially (Figure 1, 2, 3 …) then, if a new one is inserted later on, the whole document may need to be renumbered. Avoid this method if possible.

Layout

Whatever method is chosen, adopt it for the whole bid; consistency is all. Charts, figures and illustrations must also look as though they belong to the same document and come from the same, professional organization. Diagrams need to be surrounded by enough white space to separate them from the text and to make it clear where the diagram begins and ends. Diagrams should be centred on the page and printed large enough so that any text on them is clearly visible.

Design

The basics for diagrams and presentation slides are much the same. Keep it simple. Unless you have access to a professional illustrator or designer, resist the temptation to produce anything more than a basic illustration. Clip art (sample artwork provided by a software application supplier) can be a useful supplement to limited artistic skills, but it must be used with care as it was not created with your specific audience in mind, nor was it designed to go with a particular house style. For standard items such as office equipment, computers, buildings and the like this is not usually an issue. Beware of using humorous images if you are not 100 per cent sure that the client will find them funny too. There is a risk that they may think, 'if it is a joke to them now, how will they treat me after they have won the business?' In addition to clip art there are numerous drawing packages available. These require the skills of an illustrator if anything adventurous is planned, but they can be useful. They usually provide basic shapes such as rectangles and circles, and often have basic components required for flow charts and organization charts.

> *Hint.* Beware of fold-out large-scale charts. They can look very good, but will add significantly to production problems at bid delivery time. Use them only if there is a real benefit to the bid document and try to have them at the start of a section so that editorial changes do not cause havoc later on.

TABLES OF CONTENTS, INDEXES

In any document longer than about 10 pages a contents list is a useful aid to navigation. Once a document gets past 50 pages then it is almost essential. The level of detail that needs to be in a contents list varies, usually with the audience. At one end of the spectrum, typically Ministry of Defence technical procurements, it will be necessary to number every paragraph and it may even be necessary to give every paragraph an entry in the contents table. This will lead to a contents section that can run into several pages. At the other end of this spectrum a list of section headings will be enough. If the client has specified what they want, follow their instructions.

Unsurprisingly, the default choice should be somewhere in between the extremes. A typical bid document contents list should look something like the one given below. These contents cover the volumes, section and major sub-sections of a typical bid with some notes on the material that will be contained in each section. The headings are examples only, this is not a recipe for a bid.

Volume 1	*Main bid document*
1 Introduction	Brief outline of what the bid is for, why procurement is happening and so forth. This should be very short, perhaps just one paragraph.
2 Management summary	The key selling themes and messages. At least one clear diagram should be included here. Very important section, but should not be more than a few pages.
3 Understanding of requirements	Summary and details of what the bidder understands the
3.1 Summary	requirements to be. This should be in your own words and pictures,
3.2 Business	not a replay of the client's description from the tender documents.
3.3 Technical	Use diagrams and pictures to break up the text. This may be longer
3.4 Resources	than the management summary, but should be a relatively quick read.
3.5 Timetable	
3.6 Constraints	
4 Proposed solution	How the requirements will be filled. Should be similar in look, feel
4.1 Overview	and length to Section 3. Use pictures and charts to break up text and
4.2 Detail	put messages over clearly.
4.3 More detail	
5 Client requirements	Detailed list of client supplied requirements/questions (numbered as
5.1 Buildings	instructed/supplied by client together with organisation's responses).
5.1.1 Location	This could be a very long section, so reproduce client's words in small
5.1.2 Services	but readable italic type to separate them from responses. There may
5.2 Business hours	be a compliance matrix associated with this where boxes are
5.2.1 Weekdays	ticked/notes made to show that a requirement has/has not been
5.2.2 Superstores	met. This will typically be in table form.
5.2.3 Out of hours	
Volume 2	Often separated for confidentiality reasons and so as not to bias or distract those evaluating the solution.
6 Financial proposal	The pricing for the equipment/services to be offered. Broken down
6.1 Summary	and summarised to make it as easy as possible for the client to
6.2 Price breakdown	understand what is being offered and what a good deal they are
6.3 Options	getting. If this is short, bind it as a small document, don't put a few pages in a large binder as it will look silly.
Volume 3	Usually separate so it does not have to be carted around by those who do not need to look at it!

7 Annexes	Essentially anything detailed or not directly related to the bid that
A Specifications	does not belong in main body of the bid document. Summarise key
B Annual report	points from annexes or appendices in main bid as necessary to
C Terms and conditions	support sales case. Some of this material may be hard to bind, it may
D Technical stuff	be necessary to be creative about this. Get the information together
	early to see how it will fit.

Where bid documents cover multiple volumes there needs to be a contents section for each volume. It is also recommended that following this there should be the contents for the other volumes so that any cross-references that people need are made as easy as possible. In addition this lets readers see where information is covered that is not directly relevant to them at the moment.

In some cases, where sections are long (at least 20 pages) it may be worth having a detailed list in front of each section. Unless this is a customer-imposed length, it is worth asking if the section really should be so big. Would it be better split into smaller sections?

The case for indexes is less clear than for contents. Bid documents are not really like textbooks. They are more like works of fiction in that the readers need to know where they are in the story, but are unlikely to want to look for all entries referring to, say, 'software installation'. If there is an overwhelming case to have an index (the only one the author can think of is if the client insists) then plan ahead. Establish the minimum number of entries that must be included in the index and allow a large amount of time at the end of the bid for generating it.

SAMPLE PAGES

Two sample pages are offered in Figures 9.3 and 9.4 as examples of simple and effective designs that are consistent with the suggested guidelines and have been positively received by the author's clients. Figure 9.3 is the more formal one and may be better suited to government, military, health and similar markets. Figure 9.4 is less formal and should suit most commercial organizations. The latter also has the benefit of a large margin for notes and space for break-out boxes. The author has used layouts similar to this in all sectors and has received a positive response from clients. In both cases the text is aligned as ragged right and a conservative approach to different fonts and styles has been adopted.

BINDERS AND BINDING

The binder is the first thing that the client sees when receiving the bid document. If it looks cheap, amateurish or messy then you will have already reduced your chances of winning. First a choice needs to be made on how the bid will be packaged. This list gives suggestions on which to choose:

Binding method	Comments
Two-hole binder	These are readily available, and every office will have a two-hole punch; two-hole pre-punched paper is also quite common. These tend not to work so well with large numbers of pages and it is quite easy for pages to get torn. It is easy for the client to take out pages and make copies. These binders are available in many colours and can be obtained with clear plastic pouches suitable for containing covers, spines and back sheets for artwork. Where a large number of

1   MANAGEMENT SUMMARY

1.1   Introduction

This proposal documents David Nickson's proposal to Gower
Publishing for a Bid Management book. It covers the points
requested by the Editor and shows why publishing it will benefit
both Gower and David.

1.2   Key Points

Review of proposals and other bid documents has shown them to
be variable and inconsistent. Furthermore, they do not do justice
to the competent and professional staff within the organizations
that produce them.

Proposals fall short of the standard to be expected from an
organization of the calibre of BSNB. They are often repetitive,
contain simple errors, do not always answer the questions asked
and lack consistency. The client's perception can be of rather
intimidating, difficult to use and unattractive documents that lack
customer focus – in particular strong sales propositions.

*Note. David Nickson has the skills to produce excellent proposals
and explains how others can do the same. Everyone asked stated
that there were insufficient bid management books on the market.*

1.3   Way Forward

Buying David Nickson's book on Bid Management will have
major benefits to most organizations. These include:

- producing consistent bids more easily;
- winning major new business;
- reducing last minute panics to a minimum;
- making the world a better place;
- raising audiences to their feet.

Figure 9.3   *Sample management summary page (formal)*

David Nickson's   Bid Manager's Handbook Proposal   Gower

1   **Management Summary**

1.1   **INTRODUCTION**

This proposal documents David Nickson's proposal to Gower
Publishing for a Bid Management book. It covers the points
requested by the Editor and shows why publishing it will
benefit both Gower and David.

1.2   **KEY POINTS**

Review of proposals and other bid documents has shown them
to be variable and inconsistent. Furthermore, they do not do
justice to the competent and professional staff within the
organizations that produce them.

> David Nickson
> has the skills to
> produce excellent
> proposals and
> explains how
> others can do the
> same.

Proposals fall short of the standard to be expected from an
organization of the calibre of BSNB. They are often repetitive,
contain simple errors, do not always answer the questions asked
and lack consistency. The client's perception can be of rather
intimidating, difficult to use and unattractive documents that
lack customer focus – in particular strong sales propositions.

1.3   **WAY FORWARD**

Buying David Nickson's book on Bid Management will have
major benefits to most organizations. These include:

> Everyone asked
> stated that there
> were insufficient
> bid management
> books on the
> market.

- producing consistent bids more easily;
- winning major new business;
- reducing last minute panics to a minimum;
- making the world a better place;
- raising audiences to their feet.

Commercial in Confidence V1.0 08/01/02   *Page 1 of 1*

Figure 9.4   *Sample management summary page (less formal)*

	volumes and copies are involved these lend themselves well to mass-production collating parties at the end of the bid.
Four-hole binder	These are not quite as commonplace as two-hole binders and people do tend to keep their four-hole punches under lock and key. That said there should be no real problem and the benefits of not having the pages flap around so much and the impression of greater quality make these the author's choice. They are available in many colours and can be obtained with clear plastic pouches suitable for containing covers, spines and back sheets for artwork. As with two-hole binders they are suitable for mass-production techniques.
Three-hole binder	Do not use these! They are not in common use and even if your organization has the equipment to punch the holes and so on the client probably will not so will get annoyed if they want to put in material such as notes or copies of their own questions.
Plastic comb	Come in various sizes and colours capable of taking anything from just a few pages to over a hundred. These can give a good result but tend to be time consuming to use and are not client friendly in terms of disassembly for copying and so forth. Time consuming to use for large print runs and multiple volume bids. Make sure the margin is wide enough to allow for the binding – be extra careful if using double-sided printing.
Spiral wire bound	As for plastic comb, but look less attractive and are even harder to unravel. Again, make sure the margin is wide enough to allow for the binding – be extra careful if using double-sided printing.
Glue bound	Involves the use of a thermal binder in conjunction with special sleeves into which the pages are placed. Only suitable for relatively small documents as they are prone to coming apart. They are also time consuming to use for anything other than a fairly small bid, as there is little scope for mass-production techniques. Major disadvantage is that the client will find these difficult to photocopy for internal distribution. Finished product can look good, but not usually appropriate for bids. Do not forget to check the margins.

Whatever you decide, you will need to have some form of artwork for the outside of the bid document. In some organizations this is done for you – there will be a company standard folder with logo, perhaps a suitable image dreamt up by the Marketing Division. In this case, use it. As a Bid Manager you will not have time to argue about it even if you think it foul. If there is nothing available then you will have to source something from within the bid team.

Note. Make sure you have permission to use any trademarks, logos and other copyright material that you include on the cover/spine of your binder. This applies to anything you effectively publish as part of a bid.

FINISHING TOUCHES

These are in the 'nice to have' category. If time permits, they do add to the overall package, and are the sort of thing you can get organized for one bid and use as the basis for the next. Once set up they will not have the time penalty that might preclude their use. If the organization has a dedicated print room, bid production facility or similar facility (often within marketing) then it might be possible to get them to produce these sorts of things.

Bound documents

Include a clear plastic sheet (they can be obtained ready punched) in front and behind the bid document when using a binder. In the case of binders with covers, it stops the pages sticking to them. In the case of spiral/glue binds, it helps to give a smart appearance and helps keep them coffee-proof in use.

Spines

When using binders that have a clear plastic envelope on the spine, create some artwork to go in this with the client logo, organization logo, title of volume/bid and so on. This adds to the overall quality feel of the end product.

Dividers

Although these have already been identified as an essential for making the bid documents easy to use there is scope for using dividers with artwork to give a smart impression. It is even possible to have them printed with key points from the section that follows them – hammering home key sales themes. This does take time and if it has to be left until the last minute the extra hassle is not worth the effort.

Book marks

A plain bookmark will make the job of anyone evaluating your bid easier to do. There is also an opportunity to include sales messages, company logo and attractive artwork on the bookmark, which demonstrates attention to detail and puts across the idea that you care about the client. One possibility is to include a basic contents list on this, but keep it high level unless there is time to make last minute changes to it. For example, were this book to be a bid, then as well as having the Gower logo on it, it might have 'Better Bid Management Saves You Time' printed on a book mark.

Custom labels for computer disks

If an electronic copy of the bid is being included on a floppy disk, CD or DVD then it is worth having suitable pre-printed labelling or artwork to identify them. Handwritten ones look messy and failing to label them at all is asking for trouble.

Presentation material

SLIDES

As for page layout and design, the answer – unless a professional designer is to hand – is to keep it simple. Keep the number of special effects to a minimum, choose a plain background with perhaps your organization's and the client's logo discreetly placed. Use special effects such as dissolves and animation sparingly; they can look very tacky if not done well and depend on the experience and familiarity with the software presentation package used. A simple, if slightly dull, example is given in Figure 9.5.

HANDOUTS

These are to support the presentation, not to supplant it. As a minimum for any client

---

Purpose of Bid Management

- Evaluate bids prior to making the bid/no-bid decision based on risk, quality of business, resources

- Greater branding and quality of bids

- Improve chances of winning 'good' business

- Focus on costing and pricing

- Better resource utilization

- Make life easier

- Identify templates/library material

Bid Management © D. Nickson 2002

Figure 9.5   *Sample layout of a slide*

presentation this should include a hard copy of the slides. If these have used colour then consider providing the handouts in colour too. If cost is an issue, or time does not permit – colour printing often takes longer, certainly when photocopying is involved – then provide one handout in colour and the rest in grey scale. The single colour copy is required in case some of the slides only make sense if seen in colour.

Rather than print out every slide full size, one to a page, look at printing two, three or four to a page. As long as they are still readable it will save you time and reduce the bulk of the handouts. Leave space for note taking. Do this even if you do not give out the handouts until the end of the presentation; it can be helpful to the recipient later on. The author believes in giving out handouts after the presentation, as it discourages the audience from reading ahead and getting distracted.

Be careful about including anything else in the handouts; you are unlikely to be giving a presentation that is based upon a fixed script so there is no need for that. You might want to provide supporting material such as brochures, technical information and so forth. However, if it is not directly relevant to the presentation content and the audience it is probably not needed.

Style guide

Making design decisions can be difficult, because since everyone has their own aesthetic taste they all think they have a view worthy of consideration. The philosophy of the author is, 'if it looks right, it probably is right'. However, if the design decisions are to be of any use they need to be frozen and communicated to everyone that needs them. Furthermore, they need to be policed to make sure that they are put into practice. Within a bid team the Bid Manager owns the responsibility for making sure that the documents produced meet the style guide. The list below shows a suggested structure and content for a style guide for a bid document:

1	Text styles	As described earlier the agreed specification for different uses of fonts for display of the written word in a bid. For example Times New Roman, 11 point for plain text. Standards for numbering should also be included.
2	Use of logos	Rules to be applied when using the organization's and the client's logos: where they can be placed, size, permissions required and the like.
3	Page layouts	Standards for page layouts, templates for use, page size and related matters.
4	Presentation layouts	Standards and templates for slides to be used in client presentations, the use of logos and similar considerations as before.
5	Technical standards	These cover any technical constraints that need to be considered when producing anything for inclusion in a bid. For example word processing formats, acceptable formats for picture, bit map images, spreadsheets and so forth: for example, MS-Word Version 6 format, JPEG, BMP, Lotus 123 and so forth. Some of the more common ones are included in the glossary.
6	Presentation and binding	Binders to be used, covers, cover sheets, book marks, contents and similar.
7	Language and grammar	Guidelines on common errors, use of organization and brand names, capitalization, spell checkers, writing style (for example use of first or third person) and so forth.

CASE STUDY

SITUATION

Felicity S, a sales person with BS, returned from holiday to find an RFI in her in tray. This was for the first stage of a large-scale procurement and was intended to produce a long list of about 10 to 12 potential bidders. There were only four days left to turn this round, but the information was something that was often asked for so she did not think it would be too much of a problem. Felicity was not able to get hold of the usual pre-sales people who were used to working on bids but was able to obtain the appropriate technical expertise from the operational side of the organization.

PROBLEM

Nobody working on the bid was a particular expert in the use of word processing. They could all type a bit and use the spell checker, but little more than that. Furthermore there were no company standards within BS for bid documents, so there were no templates either. Given the relatively short time available they took the pragmatic option and just got on with it.

Members of the team took responsibility for answering the question that fitted with their expertise. They then typed up what they produced and the sales person cut and pasted the results together. Sadly, nobody involved had any design expertise or desktop publishing experience.

OUTCOME

The sections that were stitched together by Felicity all used different margins, type fonts and heading styles. What is more, what diagrams there were had no labels and tended to be dropped in at any old place. As a consequence the state of the BS bid document was so poor that they failed to make it past the long list stage. In part this could have been put down to bad management. However, this was not helped by a total lack of any standards for documents or anyone with any design or even desktop publishing experience being available to the bid team. This was a shame because the intellectual content was good and as an organization they should have made it to the shortlist stage, let alone the long list.

LESSON LEARNT

BS decided to invest in the design and production of a standard design and layout, complete with templates for all its client-delivered literature. This was captured in a style guide and was supported by the production of electronic templates that could be issued to those producing or working on a bid. This meant that, whoever had to work on a bid the end result would be consistent with the house style and at least have a reasonably attractive look to it.

Checklist

Item	Description	Completed?
White space	Is there enough white space to make the page look uncrowded, leave space for notes and separate pictures and diagrams from the text?	
Critical information	Every page should include the date, a title, copyright/security notice, relevant company and client information. Has this been done?	
Photocopy friendly	Does the layout allow scope for errors that occur in copying? Where colour is used does the black and white copy still make sense?	
Pages numbered	Are all pages numbered?	
Binding	Does the layout leave enough margin space to allow it to be bound, stapled or hole punched and still be readable? If double sided, does this apply to both margins?	
Style guide	Does this cover: 1 text styles? 2 use of logos? 3 page layouts? 4 presentation layouts? 5 technical standards? 6 presentation and binding? 7 language and grammar?	

3 *Personal Skills*

Part 3: Summary

Part 3 covers the 'soft' skills that a Bid Manager will find useful if the job described in Part 1 is to be done effectively. To acquire these skills needs training, time and practice. The contents of the chapters in this part of the book should be seen as a starting point; the reader may want to look out for training courses that cover individual skills in more depth. As before, checklists have been provided to help with these skills, but they cannot replace the skills themselves.

At the heart of all these skills is the ability to communicate, and that is why that subject was chosen for the first chapter in this part – all else depends upon it. If the reader is really pushed for time, and if it is being read whilst in the middle of your first bid, then make sure you at least read that chapter. See Figure P.3 for the full range of 'soft' skills.

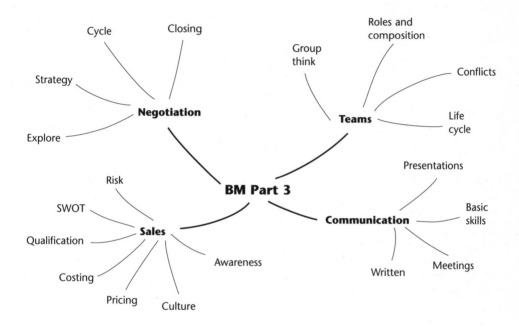

Figure P.3   *Mind Map®: Bid management, Part 3*

10 *Communication*

Good communication is as stimulating as black coffee and just as hard to sleep after.
(Anne Morrow Lindbergh, 1955)

Without strong communication skills it is very hard to manage a bid with any degree of success. This chapter provides an overview of how to communicate effectively using all the media that a Bid Manager is likely to encounter on a day-to-day basis. This chapter is not intended to replace presentation and communications training courses but to provide a health check and quick fix guide. There is a considerable amount of material here, take it slowly. The Mind Map® in Figure 10.1 shows the elements of the chapter. There is a brief overview of communications in general followed by notes on the good, the bad and the ugly of the types of communication that a Bid Manager will encounter from day to day. Think of this whole chapter as a checklist and sanity check on how you go about your day-to-day communications.

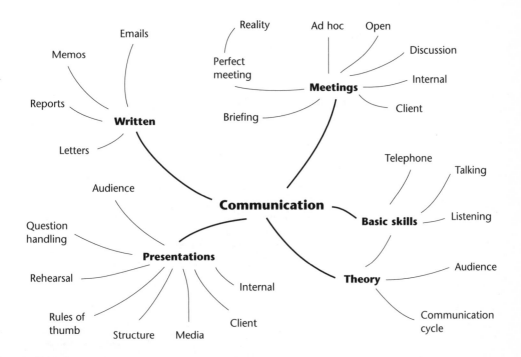

Figure 10.1   *Mind Map®: Communication*

Theory into practice

If you do not read anything else in this chapter, please read this very short section on the theory of communication. This is not an academic treatise, but a very short description of the fundamentals of all communication. What is presented here applies to all person-to-person interactions.

The communication cycle is shown in Figure 10.2.

The main aim of giving this information to readers is to make sure that they appreciate what is going on between them when deciding they want to pass on some information to another person, and whether the person is actually getting the message or not.

Aim	Needing or desiring to communicate with another person. Thoughts, objectives, internal plans, feelings and so forth.
Encode	Turning internal thoughts and/or feelings into an external means for transmission as an understandable message.
Transmit	Sending the message by spoken, written, drawn, body language, visual signal, tone of voice or other method.
Receive	Getting the message by hearing, looking, sensing and so on.
Decode	Turning the message into internal thoughts, emotions that make sense to the recipient.
Respond	Needing or desiring to respond to the message that was sent. Thoughts, objectives, internal plans, feelings and so forth.

The golden rule is that, *the message is the responsibility of the sender, not the receiver.* Communication is only effective if the information is satisfactorily received and understood.

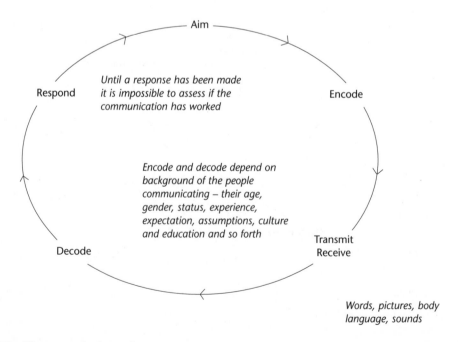

Figure 10.2   *The communication cycle*

Basic skills

The two basic communications skills needed are listening and talking, preferably in that order.

LISTENING

A good Bid Manager listens. The following is given to allow the reader to assess his or her own listening skills.

Do you:

- listen all the way through without reacting or making a pre-emptive judgement?
- ask for clarification of anything you do not understand?
- avoid interrupting except when necessary for clarification?
- take notes?
- check assumptions?
- encourage the speaker by making encouraging noises, maintaining eye contact, nodding and so on?

> *Food for thought*. Whilst listening you will need to ask questions. Try to use open questions – the type that do not have a yes or no answer, for example 'what do you think the key factors are in delivering a successful catering service to your organization?'

TALKING

Bid Managers also need to talk in order to give out information.

Do you:

- ask yourself if this is the best time to communicate this information?
- check whether there is anything that is going to distract you or your listener?
- check that you are using the best method for the information, e.g. words, pictures, and so on?
- make sure you are going at the right speed?
- check that the message is being understood as you go along?
- check if a summary is required?

To summarize:

- Decide what you wish to communicate.
- Choose the method and the medium to suit the recipient.
- Check that the recipient has understood it.

TELEPHONE

Use of the telephone is another basic skill. However popular email and text messaging become, verbal communication by telephone will remain dominant until practical and affordable videophones take over. Even then there will be many who prefer not to be seen whilst they chat. The following points are relevant to all calls, but count double for any call with the client. It is vital that all calls with clients are noted and salient points circulated within the team. Providing the handwriting is legible, there is no need to do more than photocopy notes made in a day book or on any convenient piece of paper.

For client calls the Bid Manager should encourage the team to follow this checklist:

1   Note the time and date;
2   Who the call is with;
3   Requests for information;
4   Information given;
5   Any actions requested or agreed to;
6   Any thoughts immediately after the call (do not wait) as to its importance, any new agendas, what it may mean for the bid.

Where new information is asked for or the client requests specific actions you should follow up with a request for written, or at an least email/fax confirmation of what was required. The author knows of more than one case where what was asked for on the phone was significantly different from what was later requested in writing once the client had time to think about the call. Verbal communication is not worth the paper it is written on.

Food for thought. Before you send an email, ask yourself if a phone call might work better.

Meetings

As mentioned elsewhere, a Bid Manager will be involved in a wide range of meetings and will need to be able to facilitate, participate and run them.

HOW TO RUN THE PERFECT MEETING

In theory it is very easy to have the perfect meeting. Here is the twelve step plan.

1   Make sure everyone knows when and where and that the room is booked.
2   Have the people there who need to be there.
3   Do not have anyone else there.
4   Have a reason for the meeting, goals to be achieved.
5   Have an agenda that facilitates these.
6   Item one is to agree the agenda before you start.
7   Have a chairperson who keeps things on track.
8   Take anything not directly relevant to the meeting 'off line'.
9   Take minutes.
10   Summarize actions.
11   Plan any follow-up meetings if needed.
12   Issue minutes promptly.

This really does work, and if you can stick with it you will have good and productive meetings. However, experience shows that when bids are running it becomes more and more difficult to achieve this state of nirvana. It is not easy to start with, many people resent the discipline necessary to have effective meetings, it is not any fun if you know what you are doing! Then 'events' get in the way, the person you need to make the decision is not available for the meeting when everyone else is.

Note. Keeping to the agenda will not make you popular, but it saves time. However, make sure that time is made later to cover important points that did not belong in the meeting.

REALITY CHECK

However, life is seldom like this, particularly when in the midst of a bid there are snags that prevent you from running the perfect meeting. Here are practical suggestions for dealing with the more common variations that crop up during bids. Specifically covered are the ad hoc meeting, the open discussion and the progress meeting.

AD HOC MEETING

These spring up all over the place, typically when an 'event' happens. For example, the client issues an amendment to one of the requirements or amends the procurement schedule, or the sales person receives some morsel of information that is considered critical and sets about rounding up anybody within reach to decide what to do in response to this information. Such meetings need to be kept very short as they typically result in a lot of 'sound and fury, signifying nothing'. It is all too easy to waste many hours of collective effort pulling people off productive work and ending up with nothing to show for it. The main task is to quickly establish if the new piece of information is significant or not and, if it is, determine the actions that need to be taken in order to resolve any issues. Any attempt to solve issues on the spot must be discouraged. The Bid Manager's goal is to cut these meetings short, but make sure that any key facts are captured so that they can be dealt with by the right people in a slightly more controlled, and productive, manner.

Note. It is a fine line between these ad hoc meetings and chance encounters by the coffee machine – the latter are not to be discouraged.

OPEN DISCUSSION

There will be many of these during the life of a bid and their purpose will vary. For example, one may be a brainstorming meeting to come up with an alternative solution, another to think of a better sales strategy. These meetings are both very useful and very dangerous. It is obviously necessary to give people the chance to think up better ways of doing things and have them debated within the team. However, such meetings can become 'rat holed' into a series of in-depth discussions that prevent any real progress being made. It is very easy to use up a huge amount of time without actually doing anything useful. This is a very real danger as these meetings can often seem very enjoyable to the participants. The solution to this is to have a facilitator and scribe.

The role of the facilitator is to keep things under control, a cross between a chairperson and referee. The facilitator must agree with those present what the range of topics for discussion is and use this to determine an agenda. The meeting can then be treated as for any other and things are under control.

If the meeting is a pure brainstorming one whose function is simply to come up with new ideas, then the time available should be split into sections. The first is a free-form ideas session where anything, and everything, is written down as it comes to mind – no attempt at evaluating or discussing the ideas can be allowed. The facilitator acts as controller, stopping attempts at debate. The next session is a, first cut, consider or reject debate covering the individual ideas. Everyone can have their say and ideas are accepted for further consideration by common agreement. The role of the facilitator is that of chairperson.

The role of the scribe is to write up ideas, actions and points for discussion on a flip chart or whiteboard so that they can be captured later. This leaves the other participants free to concentrate on thinking. If everyone in the meeting will be an active participant, then people should take it in turns to perform the scribe role for, say, 10 minutes or so.

It may be possible for these two roles to be combined, the Bid Manager is an obvious candidate, but only if you can read the handwriting.

It is important that the facilitator sums up at the end of the meeting. This summary should include any actions, with timings and identified deliverables, that people have agreed to complete. It should also cover any follow-up meetings and plans for further discussions that have been made.

The good facilitator:

- arrives before the meeting is due to start;
- ensures that the meeting place is as comfortable and well equipped as possible;
- introduces the agenda and helps the group to stick to it;
- makes sure that everyone knows each other;
- sticks to the time allowed;
- has no favourites;
- encourages the quieter members of the group to speak;
- summarizes regularly;
- keeps notes or appoints a scribe and makes sure that the notes are distributed quickly after the meeting;
- motivates the group to contribute by valuing their input;
- arbitrates when non-useful dissent breaks out;
- does not speak until the rest of the group has had their say;
- takes on any roles that are missing from the team (supporter, outsider, devil's advocate or leader where needed, and allows the leadership to rotate where necessary);
- makes sure that absent group members receive a copy of the meeting notes;
- makes an action list and checks that the actions on the list are completed;
- sets the time for the next meeting;
- never loses his or her temper.

Note: good facilitators are unbelievably rare.

PROGRESS MEETINGS

You need to have these for three main reasons: to make sure that the core bid team knows what is happening and where they have got to; to provide a forum for raising issues/problems (not necessarily for solving them); and to check that actions have been followed up. For distributed bid teams and those with part-time members these meetings offer the chance to meet up in person with the other members of the team.

A typical agenda for such a meeting will include: reviews of actions from the previous meeting, individual progress reports, identification of actions to be raised and their priority, agreeing any pressing issues that need to be escalated outside of the bid team for resolution, and a summary. These meetings should be as brief as possible and anything that cannot be resolved within five minutes should be resolved elsewhere (that is, it will become an action).

Good idea. One excellent idea that the author saw at one of his clients was the 'Sunrise' meeting. Although this was in a project setting, the approach would work equally well in any team environment. These meetings were held twice a week on Tuesdays and Wednesdays, and involved the entire team (except where urgent activity precluded this) and had a very simple agenda. The Bid, or in this case project, Manager went round the room and asked what each did yesterday, and what they planned to do today. The rules were that the whole meeting could take no more than 30 minutes and that attendees should stand. Issues were to be identified but, unless trivial, would be solved outside of the meeting. The Bid Manager produced a summary of what was said for circulation to all present, and those unable to be present. The meetings were scheduled to take place 30 minutes earlier than the usual start time, say 08.30, before people had got involved in the rough and tumble of the day. There were four significant benefits of these meetings:

1 Everyone knew what was going on and who was doing what, and when.
2 Clashes in timetables and missing links in work to be done became very apparent.
3 There was a positive contribution to team moral.
4 A number of problems were solved with a conversation that might otherwise have escalated into something considerably more time consuming.

There were other benefits such as the ability of people to schedule follow-on meetings knowing that everyone was in the same place at least at the start of the day, significantly reducing the logistical tasks of convening a meeting. Because the meetings involved everyone and were run on an egalitarian basis, the problem of management information filtering, where bad news gets censored, was considerably reduced. The frequency of these meetings, at twice a week, worked well for that project. Different frequencies might be considered according to the needs of the individual bid and the workload at a given time. These meetings work, they do not take up too much time, and there is undoubtedly an overall time saving to the bid.

MEETINGS WITH CLIENTS

There is always additional pressure on meetings with the client, you have to keep in mind that there is always a selling element involved. At the very least there is the risk that careless talk will cost the sale. For this reason it is very important to treat every client meeting as a sales call: there should be a briefing for all those who are to attend, plus those who need to get points put across on their behalf or need information gathered for them.

If the supplier instigates the meeting then it is reasonable to set the agenda. However, it is courteous, and can often turn up useful information, to ask the client if they want any items added to the agenda. Always make doubly sure that the client knows what type of information is being presented to them, and what information is being requested from them, well in advance of the meeting. They can then ensure that the right people are present at the meeting. If this is not done then not only is there a risk of looking unprofessional at the meeting but it may become necessary to have another meeting to complete the job – wasting time.

Every client meeting should be followed up quickly with a debrief meeting, which should be minuted to make sure everyone who needs to know can find out what went on. This meeting needs to take place before people have time to forget, or reinterpret what was actually said.

> *Note.* As mentioned in Chapter 5 on administration the Bid Manager should be keeping a list of meetings, ideally in a form, e.g. intranet, that can be accessed by all the bid team. This is very important where there are partner companies or more than one division of an organization involved. It is essential that the bidder's organization behave as an organic whole. The situation should never be allowed to occur where the same person in the client organization gets approached by two or three people for a meeting to gather the same information. Such meetings need to be co-ordinated. However, do not be tempted to take everyone along to the same meeting, as this can be intimidating for the client. Delegate one or two people to represent the others.

BRIEFING

Because bid teams are fluid and often involve specialist staff on an ad hoc basis, briefing staff is an inevitable part of the Bid Manager's job. This is not something that should be done on a casual basis by grabbing five minutes just before a meeting. If the goal is to get someone contributing effectively as fast as possible, and it invariably is if a bid is in progress, then briefing needs to be planned for. Time saved with a slipshod briefing will be more than made up for in lost time from poor productivity.

This is an area where the Bid Manager can benefit from the investment in producing the bid brief (see Chapter 3). In many cases the bid brief will cover 90 per cent of the information anyone coming into the bid will need. At the very least the bid brief can be given to those clients involved in the bid.

> *Note.* A bid brief will often contain confidential information, if you are briefing an 'outsider' then you may need to edit out anything which you do not want them to see.

TELECONFERENCES

Teleconferences are often used when it is impractical to get everyone together for a meeting. These used to be the preserve of large organizations and, even then, were looked upon as expensive as they required dedicated conference suites. At the time of writing they have become commonplace, partly because of the much reduced cost of the equipment needed. Essentially teleconferences can be treated in much the same way as meetings, and everything in terms of organization, agendas, minutes, follow-up and so forth still applies.

However there are points which need to be kept in mind:

- Time delays – with current technology the images are often jerky and there can be a delay between a gesture being made and/or a word spoken and the presentation equipment showing it.
- Image quality – this can be poor when compared with a conventional television and it is possible to miss, or mistake visual cues that would not happen in a 'real' meeting.
- Interruptions – these can occur due to glitches in the delivery technology. They may be triggered by someone joining or leaving the conference or technical events.

Time will improve this technology, indeed it is very good already, but at the time of writing it was still not as good as being physically present at a meeting. The participants need to keep in mind the limitations and make allowances accordingly. Make doubly sure that the message has been received.

Presentations

In most procurement exercises there will be presentations. The most important of these will either be to the powers that be, persuading them that your bid is worth submitting, approving and so forth, or to the client to persuade them that your ideas are the best. The Bid Manager will have a significant role to play in these presentations either as presenter or as organizer. For this reason it is important that the Bid Manager has at least a general understanding of what is involved and where the pitfalls lie. This section is here to help. Again, the communications cycle applies – consider the aim, encode, transmit, receive, decode, respond sequence at all times. This will affect the way you put your presentation together and the way you deal with any questions that may arise.

This section covers the audience, presentation structure, handling questions, use of media, rehearsals, useful rules of thumb, and the differences between internal and client meetings.

THE AUDIENCE

It is often said that you should 'know your audience' for any communication, but particularly for presentations. This is easier said than done, for unless you are presenting to people you know well and have worked with for some time then how ever much research you do you will never really 'know' your audience.

STRUCTURE

It may sound trite, but the best structure for a presentation is start, middle and end. In olden days schoolteachers would use the following incantation when priming their charges to write an essay, 'say what you are going to say, say it, say what you have said'. What follows takes this time-honoured approach one step further:

	Content	*Some examples*
The start	Tell the audience what the presentation is for, stating the objectives you have for it.	'We are here to present the techincal solution for the BS plc telephone system and will show you how it will reduce your costs by 25 per cent.'
	Say who you are, with details such as job title, role, etc. if they do not already know you – even if it is only part of the audience that is new to you.	
	Say why it is you giving the presentation, if they do not know you make sure they understand that you are qualified to do so.	
	Say what is in it for them and what you expect them to get out of it.	
	If possible show that you understand the audience's concerns.	For example, they are worried about funding the bid for the next stage because they have another bid they would like to go for.
The middle	This is where you present the evidence to back up your proposition.	
	Structure the information logically.	For example, build up staff costs from individual components within related areas such as technical, managerial, administration.
	Use words that will be familiar and meaningful to the audience.	
	Include enough detail to make the case, but unless you think most of the audience specifically wants it do not overdo this detail.	
	Give real examples to illustrate points.	
	Emphasize the relevance of the material given and the benefits to the audience.	
The end	Provide a brief summary of the key points, stress the benefits to audience.	
	Show that you have met the original objectives.	'Key objective is to obtain funding to carry on with this bid' then give key points supporting this.
	The most important part of this is the call to action – what you need the audience to do as a result.	
	Make sure the audience gets the chance to ask any questions, and answer them if time permits. If it does not, arrange a follow-up meeting to answer them later.	

Make sure nobody leaves feeling that they have been ignored, dismissed, or fobbed off.

| Repeat the call to action if the question and answer session is protracted. | 'If there are no more questions, and you still agree then we need your written approval to continue with this bid.' |

Key point. Apply the 'so what test' to any information that you include in a presentation. If there is no good answer to this question along the lines of 'the purpose of this is to ... ' or 'that means that ... ' then leave it out. It is better to have a five-minute presentation that gets the point across than spend 30 minutes rambling around the subject. Indeed, wasted time is the enemy of the Bid Manager – encourage brevity in all internal presentations.

HANDLING QUESTIONS

Although the author recommends taking questions at the end of the presentation, what is stated here applies whenever questions are dealt with. No matter how well the presentation has gone, the question and answer session can make or break the whole thing. It takes considerable discipline and practice to handle questions well. The following technique is offered – it does work. It is called **STOP**.

Share the question by repeating it. This buys thinking time and makes sure that those who were asleep or too busy thinking of their own remarks to hear it the first time round know what is happening.
Think about how you will answer the question. Do not engage mouth before brain.
Only answer the question asked. Do not get diverted into side issues or give unnecessary detail.
Please remember to check with the questioner that you have answered their question.

If someone asks a question that is genuinely irrelevant, would require the reiteration of General Relativity from first principles, or similar, then politely suggest that you talk to the questioner after the meeting. Resist any temptation to put anyone down; you are not a stand up comedian dealing with hecklers.

Hint. Where the presentation involves several presenters then the 'master of ceremonies' should act as the director for all questions, repeating them and passing them on to the relevant expert. After the question has been dealt with, the 'MC' should take control again prior to the next question. This avoids anarchy.

RULES OF THUMB

The following are generally accepted as true for any presentation that involves a combination of talking, visual aids and handouts:

- Do not have more than seven points on a slide.

- Do not include anything that is not directly relevant to the presentation.
- Get there early.
- Make sure in advance that all the equipment works.
- Make sure there are enough chairs.
- Be yourself – do not try and present in a way that is not natural for you.

MEDIA

The reason they call it multimedia is that there are so many different ones to choose from. Although there are so many available it is recommended that only the following are considered for internal presentations – flip charts, whiteboards and computer-projected slides (such as Microsoft's PowerPoint™). For client presentations, unless they are very informal, stick to the computer-based option – if you do not have a computer/projector/screen combination consider hiring one. This presupposes that you are familiar with this type of equipment. If not then it is either 35 mm slides or view foils and an overhead projector. The reasons for avoiding the 35 mm and view foil option is the time it takes to produce them, their messiness, the inconvenience of making handouts and their general lack of flexibility. The author's experience in recent years is that the portable computer rules the presentation roost.

Essentially it is being assumed that all the presentation will be made by between one and five presenters to an audience of between three and 15 or so. Whatever you choose, make sure that you can make it work on the day.

INTERNAL

Bid Managers are most likely to have to make or arrange internal presentations for two reasons: to obtain approval to bid or continue and to brief people on the bid. The Bid Manager's role in these cases is likely to be as a presenter, possibly with a co-presenter from sales or a specialist area.

> *Note.* As time is at a premium during all bids, keeping effort spent on an internal presentation is a good idea. Do not waste time on glossy handouts, fancy slides and so on. Do make sure that the presentation gets the point across quickly and effectively. However, where presenting to those whose approval you need to continue, deliver or support the bid, possibly to the client, then more gloss may be needed. This is a judgement call.

CLIENT

When presenting to clients everything said before goes double. These presentations really matter, and in some cases they are the only times that you get the chance to introduce the senior management of the respective organizations to each other.

Note. When visiting a client site to give a presentation, give some thought to how many people you take along. It is tempting to take everyone who has an interest, is senior, or may be needed to answer questions in a specialist area. Do not do this. At first sight it may look like showing commitment to the client. In reality the end result is an uncoordinated mob that can easily intimidate the client. It looks ridiculous if there are more people presenting than in the audience.

REHEARSAL

For any formal presentation to the client, and for some critical internal presentations to internal staff, it is vital that all goes well. The only way to maximize the chances of success, as with any skill, is to practise. For presentations this means rehearsals. If you can get one, try and have a rehearsal audience, even if it is just two people. The author has managed to get Red team members (see Chapter 3) to act as a suitably qualified and critical audience. Accept that this will not always be possible within the timetable of a bid, so do the best you can and do not worry too much if you cannot get an audience. Even if you only give the presentation to an empty room speaking aloud you will have a much better idea of whether or not it works and how long it takes.

The main benefits of rehearsals include helping to get over nerves, finding out if what you thought you would say actually works, getting any changes of presenter smooth, sorting out the timing and making sure it all makes sense.

The main items that need to be checked out at rehearsals are:

Location	Is it suitable? Has it got enough space/seating/ventilation/power and so on?
People	Make sure everyone who will present can attend; have separate run throughs if there are timetabling problems with senior people or those only available part time.
	Do their presentations come across well – are the points they think they are making the ones that come across?
Equipment	Is there someone available who knows how to work it? Are all the cables there? Do you have spare bulbs for projectors? Does it work?
Schedule	Does the timing work? Is the material presented in a logical order?

Key point. With any presentation, first impressions count – make the first two minutes count.

Hint. The final timings that you make in your rehearsals will tend to be shorter than the timings you get in the real thing. This is because in rehearsal you do not get interruptions, you will be up to speed, you will not have delays from getting everyone seated and attentive, and you will not have latecomers. It is a good idea to take around 10 per cent (say five minutes in a one-hour presentation) off the allocated time and use that as the target. That way you will probably finish on time; even if you come to the end a couple of minutes early you can use it for question time. The cardinal sin is overrunning.

Written communication

As was established in the chapter about administration, there is a significant amount of paperwork involved in any bid. The Bid Manager needs to know how to communicate effectively in writing.

REPORTS

These will be thrust upon the Bid Manager and may take many forms. Reports will vary from a simple requirement to say what you have spent this week, up to a detailed project progress report complete with sales forecast, win probability, analysis of competition, who has done what, who will do what next week and the size of your parking space. Most of these will be defined by the organization that owns the bid and it will be a case of filling in the boxes.

However, whatever form the report takes the normal basics of communication will apply. So remember to consider the following questions:

- Who will read it, and why (know your audience)?
- Why are you writing it (even if the answer is, because you have to!)?
- What information must you get across (if there is not a space on the form, add a note)?
- What is the best structure (unless it is specified already)? If none is supplied then follow a similar format to a presentation.

> *Hint.* If there is no requirement for you to write any form of progress report on your bid, then you might consider asking why not? Even if it is only to protect your own back, there may be value in producing some kind of weekly report. The focus required to do this can well have benefits such as spotting adverse trends.

EMAIL

It is easy to get addicted to emails; something that can be sorted out with a five-minute conversation can build into an extended and increasingly acrimonious exchange of emails over a period of hours or days. Misunderstandings that would be quickly resolved face to face can take many exchanges to resolve by email. What is worse, once people get the email habit they start using it even when the person they want to communicate with is sitting in the same office. It is a good idea to think whether or not an email is the best way of getting the job done. Would a phone call or walking across the office get things done more quickly?

> *Hint.* There is one piece of advice that should be emblazoned on every email system front page: do not send the email until you have read it at least twice. It is all too easy to type in anger then repent at leisure with emails. Do not forget that emails can count for libel, if nothing else.

LETTERS

Specifically this covers writing formal letters to the client to accompany the bid itself, requesting clarifications, asking for information, asking for changes to timetable and so on.

Letters are always very important because they present the image of your organization to the client in a tangible and very visible way. Also, the recipients of a letter will have plenty of time to look at it, think about it and judge it.

As before, the first thing to consider is the audience. Who will read it? What do you want them to do as a result? As a minimum include the following information in any letter that is sent out from a bid team: date, contact details with phone, fax and email numbers as needed, the recipient's name, the sender's name, a heading which makes it clear what it is about, a unique reference number, and information that may be legally required such as a company registration number.

> *Hint.* Letters also present an opportunity. Whereas some people are perfectly happy not to return a phone call, or sometimes an email, they are much less likely to ignore a letter. Indeed, in the case of formal government procurements, letters may have to be acknowledged and their receipt recorded. So, whenever you need to write a letter to the client – it may only be to accompany submission of requested information – the chance is there for you to put across a sales point. For example, suppose you have been asked to submit copies of your company's registration and VAT certificates. You have the opportunity to include a covering letter pointing out how long you have been in business, particularly if the competitors have not.

MEMOS

As with letters, the best advice is to keep memos short and only address items that need action. In many cases it may be quicker and easier to send an email. However, where you are dealing with organizations that do not have a strong email culture there may well be a strong memo culture. Essentially what was said for emails applies – who it is for, what needs to be in it and so forth. In such organizations it is often as well to consider the politics of who you do/do not include on a memo. It is easy to cause offence by leaving someone out, even if they have nothing directly to contribute. As with emails, read all memos carefully before you send them out. Ten copies of a stupid mistake can have a big impact.

CASE STUDY

SITUATION

Susan K was the sales person for NB plc in a campaign to win a network installation for a shipping and distribution company. NB specialized in the supply of such equipment and was always able to offer an attractive deal based upon price or scheduling the supply so that the client could implement the network in a way that made their business continue to operate smoothly through a period of change. The sales culture in NB was very strong and there was a firm belief that to win business you needed to explore every possible angle to come up with the one that would swing the deal with the client. This strategy had been relatively successful in the past. Whilst this bid was larger than most worked on previously, it was by no means of such a value that it merited special consideration. However, it was more complex than most and required a significant custom element to be designed. This meant that the technical support staff, who did not often get involved other than to field specific enquiries, had to produce a significant part of the bid along with their technical design.

PROBLEM

The technical design team were not used to

working in the sales environment, and the sales team were not used to involving them in their discussions. A kick-off meeting was held, and the technical part of the client's requirements was neatly separated out for the design team to respond to. It was assumed that they would come up with a solution and cost it out. Sales would then put any spin needed on the proposal to keep it in line with the approach they settled upon with the client. To this end Susan held regular meetings with the client and brainstorming meetings with other sales staff to come up with an approach that would best suit the client. These meetings would run for hours and cover endless flip charts with different strategy options, the best of which were then discussed either formally, or informally, with the client to gauge opinion. This was the normal sales routine at NB and had a reasonable degree of success. What was different this time was that the technical part of the bid would affect the deal. They were not just shipping product and installation services but had to design something from scratch. Susan felt comfortable that the technical staff would get on with things and did not need to be distracted with the sales strategy. Anyway, they always got bored if you made them sit in on the brainstorming sessions.

OUTCOME

The bid that was submitted lacked cohesion; there were different emphases in different sections of the proposal. For example, the technology section underlined the idea of getting the solution up and running as quickly as possible so as to allow the benefits to be realized as soon as possible.

Unfortunately, the management summary, written after the last meeting, made much of the concept of a phased approach allowing each new service to bed in before introducing yet another new change. So, one message contradicted the other. They failed to make the shortlist and what should have been a good chance at a significant opportunity in familiar territory. Susan was blamed for this, but her track record helped her keep her job. She asked the client why they failed to make the shortlist and was told that, 'although both approaches were attractive, they were looking for a supplier that would provide leadership, not one that was schizophrenic'.

LESSON LEARNT

Failing to control the multiplicity of meetings that were continually trying to come up with 'the winning strategy' had led to a situation where the different contributors to the bids were working to different scripts. Worse, the time taken up in these rambling, uncontrolled meetings had significantly reduced the time available to do productive work. The balance between creativity and practicality had gone too far askew. Susan realized that the fault was largely her own. She had not done anything to keep discussions under control – she had enjoyed them – or to make sure that changes in tack were communicated to the whole team. In future she would make sure that meetings were properly controlled and minuted, and that everyone was kept informed of the strategy. Use of a bid brief (see Chapter 3) would have gone a long way to solving the problem.

Checklist

Item	Description	Completed?
Communications	Decide what you wish to communicate. Who is your audience/recipient? Have you chosen the best method for that audience? Have you chosen the best medium? Have you checked that the message was understood?	
Email	Who is it to? Sending – have you read it first? Do you still want to send it as it is? Have you remembered any attachments?	
Briefing	Briefing document available? Time and date noted? Any follow-up required? Questions answered?	
Meetings	Is the room booked? Are people notified? Agenda agreed? Facilitator needed? Minutes taken? Actions noted? Minutes/actions circulated?	
Presentations	Who is the audience? Does the presentation take this into account? Do they know when/where/why? Is the structure appropriate? Room booked? Equipment checked? Slides prepared? Handouts prepared? Enough rehearsals? Follow-up actions?	
Letters/memos	Who is it to? Proofread? Circulation? Any follow-up required?	
Telephone	For client/key calls: Time and date? Who was it with? Requests for information noted? What information was given? Any actions agreed to/made? Follow-up needed?	
Teleconference	Equipment booked? Room booked? Are you aware of time delays/equipment restrictions, and will you take account of them? Allowed for time zone issues if international? Follow-up actions?	

11 *Teams*

No one can whistle a symphony. It takes an orchestra to play it. (Halford E. Lucock)

The definition of a bid used for this book is 'an approach to a client in order to gain significant new or repeat business'. Because of this it is almost inevitable that a team will be involved in producing such a bid. This chapter looks at the composition of a bid team and, more importantly, the nature of working in teams and the opportunities and pitfalls that exist for the Bid Manager. The information presented here is intended to provide the Bid Manager with food for thought and pointers towards making the bid team work. It is not meant to be a complete guide to working in teams. Anyone looking for a more in-depth treatment is referred to the Additional Reading section at the end of the book.

The Mind Map® in Figure 11.1 shows what is covered in this chapter on teams.

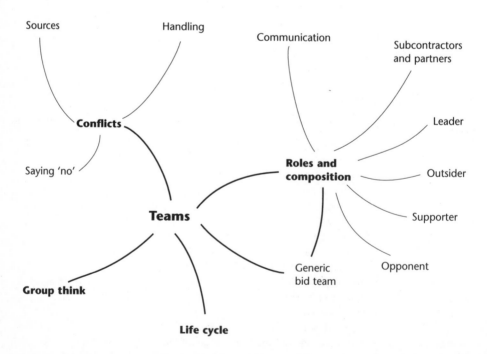

Figure 11.1 *Mind Map®: Bid teams*

The generic bid team

Figure 11.1 shows a generic bid team that is typical of those found in most organizations, independent of industry sector. In most cases the team will report into a sales function, although some companies may have it reporting into a project management, finance or commercial area. The work roles of these people are discussed in Chapter 2 and their exact function will vary from industry to industry. However, any bid team is likely to contain people with specialist skills, people dealing with the client and people who look after the commercial and legal aspects of the proposition. They will have to work together in a bid team if a bid is to be produced (Figure 11.2).

Figure 11.2   *Composition of a generic bid team*

The team will comprise people who have very different approaches to business in particular and life in general. Just think of the stereotypical images that come to mind when you think of sales people, lawyers, accountants, engineers and middle managers. How well do you think they are all going to get on? Bid teams, because of the wide variety of skills they have to include, are more diverse than almost any other project team, so the Bid Manager needs to have highly developed team-working skills.

> *Key point.* It is likely that few, if any, members of the bid team would be under the direct authority of the Bid Manager when doing their 'day jobs', they will not be direct reports. The Bid Manager often has responsibility without power and so, must often manage by consensus.

The life cycle of a team

There is a well-established life cycle for the team that describes what happens when a team is brought into being, or when its composition changes. It is often referred to as the Forming, Storming, Norming and Performing model (Figure 11.3).

The model is summarized thus:

Forming
: This happens when the team first gets together. People will mill about getting to know one another and will all ask questions about what they are supposed to be doing, why are they here, why me and so on.
At this stage the best thing a Bid Manager can do is to give strong direction. Have an induction pack, better still a bid brief. Set up a kick-off meeting and make sure that the team know what they are bidding for, and why, sort out the logistics such as desks and phones, team meetings, communications channels and so forth. The

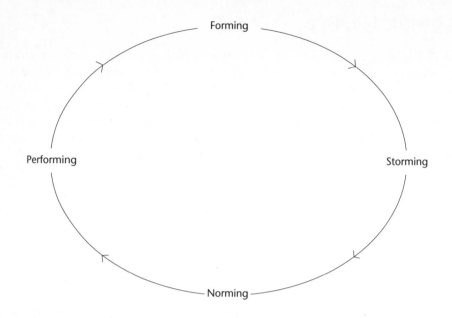

Figure 11.3 *The Forming, Storming, Norming and Performing model*

	Bid Manager needs to set objectives, discuss them with the team members and get them accepted. It is worth doing this both verbally and in writing to get the message across and to set a baseline.
Storming	The team members now know what they are doing and what their role is going to be. They now move on to questions such as who will be the leader/boss, what is my status/position, where do I fit within the team and so forth.
Norming	The team starts to come together as a unit. At this stage group 'norms' become established. These are the unwritten and unspoken 'rules' that govern the way the team behaves. Typically these include such things as style of dress, punctuality, socializing outside working hours, levels of formality and so forth. In some ways this can be looked at as being the culture of the team.
	The Bid Manager, if established as the leader, should become more of a participant than a director. However, it is usually the case that the leader's behaviour will rub off on the team. For example, if the leader is consistently late for meetings then that will probably become the norm for the team. Consequently, the Bid Manager should be careful about the example set.
Performing	This is the stage you are aiming for. The team is now spending the majority of its time actually working towards the goal of producing the bid.

Note: whenever the team changes any of its core members this whole cycle will be restarted. It may be abbreviated, but it will happen. The Bid Manager must take this into account and reset expectations on delivery accordingly. For this reason Bid Managers will resist changes to the team during a bid.

Because of the volatile nature of a bid team, and the relatively short lifetime for most bids, it is inevitable that the team spends a considerable amount of time in the early, less productive, of these phases. Consequently, the Bid Manager needs to facilitate people both coming into and out of the bid team. Time will always be at a premium and, as well as making sure that people can contribute as soon as possible, it is important to make sure that those who leave have left behind all the information needed to make use of their contribution after they have gone.

Key point. Because people come and go, having an efficient induction process is vital for making a bid team productive. A comprehensive but concise bid brief is a good starting point for this.

Team roles and composition

The Bid Manager needs to be aware that within a successful team every team member fulfils two purposes. One is what they need to do to deliver the bid (for example an engineer may need to design the technical solution). The second is their role within the team. This latter refers to the behaviours shown by the team members, how they operate within the team itself. Psychologists have identified many ways of defining team roles and individual behaviours within them and there are many excellent books on the subject (see Additional Reading). Here is a simple, and practical, approach based upon four roles that will meet the needs of the Bid Manager.

To be successful teams need to have people within them who will fill the following roles either on a full-time basis or part time.

- leader;
- opponent;
- supporter;
- outsider.

This applies to small teams as well as large ones – if you look at a team with just three people in it you will find that all the roles are still being filled.

LEADER

Every team needs a leader to give it direction. Without this role the team will produce nothing of value. Indeed, typically they will not get beyond the 'storming' stage described earlier. It is worth noting that the leader may change as the function of the team changes. For example, in the very early stages of a bid the leader may be the sales person, the team may well consist of just sales and one or two support staff. Then, when the bid team increases in size, a dedicated Bid Manager may take over the day-to-day running of the team, leaving sales to concentrate on the client campaign.

Note. At first sight it might seem reasonable that the Bid Manager would be the leader in a bid team. However, this is by no means always the case. Where the bid team reports to a sales manager/sales function then it is quite likely that sales will feel that their 'ownership' of the client and the sales strategy gives them overall control. This can give rise to conflicts between the bid team and the sales function. Then the Bid Manager needs to work closely with sales to keep things running smoothly by making sure that roles and responsibilities are clearly defined. Similar problems can arise with financial, commercial and operational management whose goals may conflict with those of the bid team.

OPPONENT

If a team is to be successful, it needs people within it who will question what is being done. Failure to do this leads to complacency and increases the chances of work being done one way, 'because it was done that way last time'. The Bid Manager must make sure there is someone to take on the role of 'devil's advocate', perhaps taking it on as part of the job. One way of doing this is to have a meeting once a week with the specific objective of challenging the status quo.

> *War story.* The author has seen the role of the opponent justified many times. One example concerned the use of 'boiler plate answers' where a client's requirement was answered with text from a previous bid where a different client had asked a similar question. Although the questions were essentially the same, their significance to the two clients was very different. A member of the bid team reading the draft was uncomfortable with the stock answer and questioned it. When the question was re-evaluated in the light of its context it became clear that the boiler plate answer was inappropriate and would have damaged the credibility of the whole bid.

SUPPORTER

These are the people who actually get the work done, if you have not got them in the team then little will actually be produced. The only point to consider is that too much uncritical obedience can be a bad thing. This is particularly true when a bid team member focuses too much on what they do and not enough on what the client may want.

OUTSIDER

These people are difficult. They can appear aloof, and may seem to have a negative impact on the team. However, they are essential as they act as quality control for the bid team. They will provide perspective and will help assess the impact of the bid on the rest of the organization. For example, they will help spot where the approach being taken by the bid team in solving the client's problem is inconsistent with the way the organization normally operates.

SUMMARY

Remember that individual team members will often fill more than one of these roles. The author often finds himself acting as a leader, a supporter and an outsider. Do not get bogged down trying to pigeonhole team members, but do look around to check that all the roles are present. If you think one is missing then do something about it. For example, if there is nobody functioning as an outsider then look for one, ask someone outside the team to review the bid.

Subcontractors and partners

Sub contractor and partner companies often contribute to bid teams. This may be in the form of documents written in response to specific questions from the client or it may involve full- or part-time involvement of third party staff. In general terms this presents no more problems than any other team member does. However, there are considerations relating to different corporate cultures, competing priorities, confidentiality and so on that the Bid Manager must allow for. Take extra time to make sure that third party staff are effectively briefed, have access to the facilities they need and, where necessary, do not have access to information you do not want them to see. Remember that they may be working with you on this bid, but against you on the next, or on another one that is going on in the next room.

Hint. Subcontractors and partners can be a useful source of 'outside' opinion. It is well worth taking time to canvas their views as to how the bid is going, what they think the client wants and so forth. This can act as a sanity check, and can provide some revealing insights into the strengths and weaknesses of your own organization.

Communication within a team

The mechanics of communication, the communication cycle of aim, encode, transmit, receive, decode and respond are just the same within a team as they are in any other environment. This is covered in more detail in Chapter 10, but the salient points can be summarized as follows:

Decide what you wish to communicate, for example a key theme for the bid.
Choose the method and the medium to suit the recipient, for example a team meeting with supporting notes.
Check that the recipient has understood it. Question the audience what they think the theme is.
Then remember that the golden rule is that *the message is the responsibility of the sender, not the receiver.* Communication is only effective if the information is satisfactorily received and understood.

It is important that the Bid Manager makes sure that all members of the team are kept up to date and have a common understanding of what is happening at any given time.

ALLOCATING WORK

As discussed earlier, a Bid Manager may, or may not, have direct control over the people working on the bid. However, whatever the situation, the Bid Manager will need to allocate tasks, activities, jobs or whatever you wish to call them to the bid team. It is important that these are communicated very efficiently to the team, as there is little or no time available to rectify mistakes. To this end it is a good idea to apply the SMART test to any work being allocated as part of the bid. In Chapter 3 the concept of the bid brief was introduced as a method of documenting who does what. That is an excellent way of communicating the basic information but it does not provide a check on whether or not the allocation of the work is sensible. SMART will fill that gap:

Simple   An instruction to answer a particular question asked by the client is simple (the answer itself may not be) and well defined.

Measurable	How will you know when it is done? For example, a complete estimate for delivery and installation requires a price and a date.
Achievable	With the resources, technology and equipment available can it be done? If you decide that your bid is to include coloured diagrams and photographs, it is essential that you have a colour printer available.
Realistic	Even if it is achievable, is it realistic to use the resources available to do it?
Timetable	Is it clear by when it needs to be completed?

It should be kept in mind that, particularly with technical questions, the Bid Manager will not necessarily know if the work required to deliver part of a bid is trivial or unrealistic. Acceptance of the tasks to be done together with agreement that they are 'SMART' is an essential sanity check. By communicating such requests to the team as early as possible, it will become clear where the problems in the bid are.

Conflict

Put people together and sooner or later there will be conflict. Bid Managers work in a relatively high-pressure environment where significant amounts of money are at risk and there will be a large number of people with oversized egos. So expect a considerable amount of conflict handling to go with the job.

SOURCES

There are many possible causes of conflict, but just as there are only a few plots for a story they usually boil down to one of the following: assumptions, communication, priority, speed and status, all expanded as follows:

Assumptions	Everybody makes assumptions whether they know it or not. Unless you check on other people's you cannot be sure that they are the same as yours.
For example at a review meeting to discuss progress the sales manager was very agitated and wound up and became increasingly cross with the bid team who seemed to be quite relaxed about progress. It turned out that the client had told her that the date for submission of the bid had been brought forward by a week. Her assumption was that the rest of the team knew about this. They did not and so did not understand her anxiety. The conflict was resolved once everyone was working from the same information. Then they could all panic together.
Communication	Unless this is perfect there is always the danger that either you or the other party is working from incomplete or misunderstood information.
The classic example here is arranging to meet someone but failing to specify the exact details. You wait outside a railway station for quarter of an hour whilst the person you were meeting was in the ticket office all the time.
Priority	Your priority may not be the same as the other person's. This often happens where people working on a bid have other 'day' jobs to do as well.
For instance, you need an operations manager to attend a meeting with the client to explain how your company ensures the smooth running of IT services. This is a major concern for the client and for you – the whole sale depends on the client having faith in your company's reliability. The operations manager cancels at the last minute because of the need to sort out a major problem and maintain service to an existing customer.

Speed	Different people work at different speeds and different personalities have different approaches to taking on new information. This does not relate to how hard people are working or how quickly they can complete a task. It concerns the time it takes them to make a decision or to accept a change.
	For instance, person A might be someone who needs to consider all the details and review all the available material before they are comfortable with a course of action. Person B may be an individual who 'shoots from the hip' and is happy to take up a new idea at a moment's notice. If these people work together there will inevitably be clashes. In a bid this is most likely to come from the interaction of sales and technical staff.
Status	This also covers territory. It relates to physical space, ownership of ideas, money, power, a desire to keep information secret, perceived position in the pecking order and so on. It is probably the easiest source of conflict to understand.
	Using another person's desk whilst they are in a meeting can be a cause of major irritation. Bid Managers who have people working part time on bids need to make sure that there are facilities for part-time team members to use, e.g. a 'drop-in desk'. This is particularly true if the part-time contributors are very senior and, so, feel that their time and contribution are very valuable and they have a right to evict more junior staff.

Bid Managers need to be aware of these sources of conflict and, where possible, put things in place that will reduce their likelihood. Good briefing will go a long way towards reducing the chances of conflict arising from assumptions and communication-related issues.

CONFLICT HANDLING

However well the Bid Manager tries to put things in place to avert conflict, it will still occur. As stated at the beginning of this section, the bid environment is one that tends to lead to conflict. Consequently, it is useful to know about the basic strategies available for dealing with conflict. The three most common are aggressive, which is based around I win/you lose; passive, where you put it off or compromise; and assertive, where the idea is to find a solution that is good for both sides.

Aggressive	Here there is no negotiation, no attempt to consider if the solution is the right one, is fair and so on. The goal is simply to win the conflict. This results in a transaction where one side wins and the other loses (a win/lose transaction). This may result in a short-term gain, but will build up resentment for the future and could well instigate the start of a tit-for-tat series of battles in which each party tries to win at the expense of the other. If this is going on in the middle of a bid then the vital focus on the client will be lost and significant time will be wasted. This is very bad news. There can be times when such a strategy is justified, for example where the client has stipulated that something must be done, or where it relates to something such as health and safety in the office. In general this strategy should be avoided.
Passive	The put-it-off or compromise solution. Possibly the worst strategy as it always leads to both sides losing (a lose/lose transaction). Nobody gets what they want and the conflict will recur. However, it may be useful where people are at each other's throats as it gives them time to cool off. It is then possible to adopt one of the more positive strategies.

Assertive

This is often considered to be the best strategy as it provides a solution that represents a win for all concerned and the conflict is unlikely to recur. The downside is that compared to the other strategies it requires more work. The following steps need to be taken in order to achieve a good result:

1 Define the problem. Concentrate on what has actually happened, not what people think should have happened. Get as precise a definition as possible. Do not let people get involved in name calling or personal attacks, keep things as dispassionate as possible. Make sure that everyone involved gets to put their case forward then summarize what the situation is. Ask for clarification if you are not sure of anything, but do so in a positive way that does not make anyone feel stupid. You cannot resolve a conflict if you become part of it.

2 What is the cause? The key issue here is to find the cause and not to blame someone for starting the conflict. As before, everyone needs to have their say and feel that they are being included. When looking at cause it is important to sift out anything that is not directly relevant to the case, such as personal dislike.

3 Find a solution. First get both sides of the conflict to say what is the outcome they want. Next you should look at any positive solutions that present themselves to you. Keep in mind that any solutions must be achievable within the constraints, such as timetable and resource availability, that may exist. As a result of the earlier work on definition and cause, those involved should be more reasonable and objective by now. Put forward the solution as a positive outcome. Where you need to make a trade-off between those involved explain it as, 'if they do this for you, then I'll get that done'. Make it clear that there is a solution to the problem that will satisfy everyone. It is very unlikely that there is not.

4 Implement the solution. Produce a plan that people sign up to. This must have clearly identified activities, a sensible timetable and be agreed to by all involved. Revisit this if necessary to make sure that everyone knows what has been done and is still happy with it.

In practice the Bid Manager will need to use all of these strategies from time to time. However, the author's experience, and the accepted wisdom, is that the assertive strategies work the best. If at all possible try and resolve a conflict with a 'win/win' solution. In the world of the Bid Manager you will inevitably need to work with these people on the next bid or they will need to work together on another one. It is worth putting in the time to get a real solution, however tempting the short cuts offered by other strategies may be.

War story. The author was working on a bid where there were three sales people. One of these had a distinctive and enthusiastic personality that was combined with a desire to cross every 't' and dot every 'i'. The occasion was a presentation to the client of the bidding company's thoughts on meeting their requirements. The conflict arose because of the enthusiasm of the sales person to tie down the last detail of a particular aspect of the proposed solution. Sadly, one of the main decision makers in the audience was someone who liked strategic rather than detailed thinking. What is more, unbeknown to the presenter, this person had a train to catch. The presentation overran whilst the enthusiastic sales person discussed more and more detail, ignoring the obvious fidgeting of a significant part of the audience. The decision maker missed his train and was distinctly chilly in subsequent meetings.

SAYING 'NO'

Related to conflicts is saying 'no'. Bid Managers are subject to reasonable, and unreasonable, demands from a wide variety of sources. It will not be possible to satisfy all of these, so a skill the Bid Manager needs to have is that of saying 'no'. If a Bid Manager does not learn to say 'no' to unreasonable demands then the following outcomes are likely:

- The bid team would become overloaded and be unable to deliver the bid.
- Delivery timetable would become a joke.
- Important tasks needed to deliver the bid would get pushed aside.
- Quality and consistency of the bid would suffer.

The way you say 'no' matters, unless the intention is to annoy people and build up resentment. The following three strategies have been found to work well:

- Use a pleasant tone of voice and just say no, firmly. There is no need to apologize when you say no, nor do you need to explain unless there is a professional reason to do so.
- As before but explain the reasons why you are saying no.
- Again, say no, give your reasons and offer an alternative. Still keep the pleasant but firm tone of voice.

For example, you may be asked by a senior manager to drop your bid for the next couple of days and get the team to help out on another bid that is in trouble. Assuming that this is an unreasonable request then saying 'no' might go something like this: 'Can't help you today, the team has to make a presentation to the client tomorrow and must rehearse. You might try the Manchester office, one of their Bid Managers has just finished a bid and may be able to help.'

> *Key point.* Assertion not aggression. Related to saying 'no' is the difference between assertion and aggression. People who are aggressive base their approach upon having nothing but contempt for others – they can only get their way at the expense of others. In any team environment this is counter-productive. However, assertion is based upon valuing yourself and those you transact with. The basis for assertion is communicating what you want done, how you feel about it and how important it is to you, whilst also taking into account how it will affect others and how important it is to them. The goal is to get things done in a positive manner. Assertion involves consensus, aggression does not.

Group think

WHAT IS IT?

'Group think', sometimes called 'team think', adversely affects seemingly successful groups. The first people to identify it were Janis and Mann who published their findings in the early 1970s. They identified that teams with group think ultimately fail because a pattern of behaviour develops which leads to poor quality decisions being made, combined with a growing isolation of the team from its surrounding environment.

They identified that groups at risk had these circumstances in common:

- They enjoy working together and are well bonded.
- They have little or no exposure to outside comment or criticism.
- No alternative plans are made or considered.
- There is pressure to make decisions very quickly.
- Strong and actively supported leadership is evident.
- No reviews are taken of decisions made/actions taken.

Bid teams can take it as read that they will make decisions very quickly, the core team will also become strongly bonded because they have to work under pressure. Also, it is quite easy for the team to escape from external criticism because nobody wants to get sucked into the world of bidding. This can be exacerbated because of the natural tendency of sales management to protect what it sees as its own patch. Consequently there are several factors running together that make bid teams prone to group think. This is particularly true for a team working on a related series of bids. Bid Managers should look for the following symptoms:

False sense of unity	The team believes that everyone within it is in complete agreement with what actions are being taken, goals pursued and so on. Silence is taken as agreement.
Self-censorship	Team members censor their own doubts to keep the team in agreement.
Pressure on dissenters	Anyone who expresses doubts will be encouraged to conform.
Justification	Members will justify any action the team takes. These justifications will often sound like rationalizations to an outsider.
Guards	Some members of the team will try actively to prevent other team members from 'rocking the boat'.
Lack of ethical considerations	The team will fail to take account of ethical considerations where these clash with what the team chooses to do.
Sense of invulnerability	The team believes it cannot fail. Symptoms of this include unjustifiable optimism, and increased risk taking.
Cartooning	Anyone outside of the team, particularly anyone critical of the team or competing with it, are treated as if they are a 'cartoon character' and dismissed as being irrelevant or unreal.

HOW TO AVOID IT

The best antidote to group think is a review process. The team needs to have its views checked, either by an individual within the group who acts as an outsider – someone taking on the role of devil's advocate for example – or by an external person or group. The review or Red team (see also Chapter 3) can fulfil this function. What often keeps bid teams from the fate of group think is the volatility of the team and the short timetable and changing requirements imposed by the client. However, the Bid Manager should check for symptoms of this as part of the role, particularly when working with a team that has produced a series of successful bids. The effects of group think on a bid are usually disastrous.

CASE STUDY

SITUATION

BS plc were bidding for a national infrastructure project, a significant and high-profile opportunity in their home market. They were considered to be one of the favourites to win this business as they had considerable technical expertise in the field and had an in-depth appreciation of the problems involved in supplying such an infrastructure. They were competing against a number of organizations that were similar to themselves in many ways, although some were in partnership with management consultancy specialists. This project was to be the first of three in a substantial infrastructure programme. The overall size of the programme was such that it was likely that there would be more than one supplier involved, but it was expected that whoever won this first component would be well placed in the race for the remainder. Consequently, BS were to invest a significant amount of time and money in bidding for this business.

PROBLEM

The problem was that BS plc did not realize that it had a problem. BS plc considered that the key to the sale was solving the complex technical problem that they perceived the infrastructure project to be. They put together a bid team with a strong technical group that included many of BS's best industry experts. They even flew in specialists from the parent company who remained on site for the duration. They were determined to produce the best solution for the technical problem. The bid team worked very hard to achieve this in the limited time available. Indeed, one of the clues to their misconception was the limited time available, their technical team leader said that, 'the client's timetable is incompatible with such a complex problem, they can't understand what they are asking!' Nobody thought to question the sales strategy of

solving the technical problem, even when it seemed almost impossible within the timetable. Indeed, anyone who did suggest that there might be a better approach was shouted down very quickly. More technical effort was applied and the midnight oil was burnt in substantial quantities. By the time the bid was due in an impressive and complex technical design had been completed together with an in-depth proposal detailing how it all worked. The bid, as submitted, was a weighty and technical tour de force.

OUTCOME

Unfortunately, the client was not expecting a complete technical solution and BS lost this bid at an early stage, a major blow to their esteem as they would expect to have made the shortlist 'by right'. This result was quite a surprise and a debriefing meeting with the client was requested. This was doubly important as internal recriminations along the lines of, 'it was your departments fault', were quick to spring up. It was vital that the root cause of the problem was established so that remedial action could be taken and confidence restored. After all, this bid had been put together by BS's industry experts in their own field, where they were considered a market leader and had expended a significant amount of effort. Not to make the shortlist was a major blow. The client was happy to agree to the debrief meeting as it was disappointed that BS had performed so badly. This was because they had hoped that BS would be bidding for the other elements on the national infrastructure that would be required to complete the entire programme.

The debrief meeting revealed that, whilst the client had been impressed by the in-depth technical solution proposed that was not what they had expected. They were looking for a starter solution that could be implemented quickly and used as a building block for the future. Furthermore, they were looking for something that would enable them to start delivering to their customer as fast as possible. The key drivers for them were speed, visibility and ease of implementation. The complex and ingenious solution, offered by BS plc, was none of these things. Consequently, BS plc was rapped over the knuckles by the client for having woefully misunderstood what was wanted.

Although nobody used the term 'group think', that is effectively what had happened here. The BS bid team had determined that the key to the sale was a brilliant and innovative technical solution. This went unchallenged, even when the timetable made this seem impossible. The bid team had focused on the wrong problem. What the client had wanted was a practical starting point that they could use to kick-start their infrastructure programme and get things moving. They did not want the perfect technological solution at this stage; they just wanted something that would work well enough. Their goals were political and publicity related and they realized that they would need to revisit the technology as they progressed with the later phases of the programme. BS's real problem was that nobody within the team challenged the goal they were pursuing. They were victims of group think.

LESSON LEARNT

BS took the lesson to heart, in a related procurement for another infrastructure building block that took place some months later. The new sales manager put in charge of this campaign was recruited from a major competitor especially for the purpose. His major strength was not in the technology and engineering side of the industry. His brief was to make sure that the sale was firmly aimed at meeting the client's business, commercial and publicity goals with a safe and comprehensible solution. The BS bid for the next element of the client infrastructure was more successful.

Whilst this was a positive step, in that BS was listening to its client, it represented at best a partial solution to the problem. The real lesson to be learnt is that the sales strategy and focus of a bid team needs to be challenged from outside the team. This can be done by some form of review process, for example see Chapter 3 on Red teams, or by those responsible for signing off the bid before it is submitted to the client. The key point is that the strategy is tested.

Checklist

Item	Description	Completed?
Team roles	Does your team include people in the following roles: A leader? Opponents? Supporters? Outsiders?	
Conflict	Assertive conflict handling checklist. Have you: Defined the problem? Identified the cause? Found a solution? Implemented it?	
Group think	Check for: False sense of unity?	

	Self-censorship? Pressure on dissenters? Justification? Guards? Lack of ethical considerations? Sense of invulnerability? Cartooning of people outside team?	
Work allocation	When allocating tasks do they meet the SMART requirement? Simple? Measurable? Achievable? Realistic? Timetable?	
Job descriptions	Do all team members have defined roles and responsibilities?	

12 *Negotiation*

Whenever two people meet there are really six people present. There is each man as he sees himself, each man as the other person sees him, and each man as he really is. (William James)

Negotiation is a core skill for any Bid Manager. The job inevitably involves continual negotiation and renegotiations of resource, facilities, timetable and equipment. It will also include a degree of negotiation with the client, although this will be about the conduct of the bid rather than the sales proposition. It is not the intention to turn bid and/or project managers into sales staff, this is not a sales training manual, but to provide the skills needed to run a bid as smoothly as possible. As well as the usual case study there are a number of examples in this chapter that are typical of the negotiations that a Bid Manager becomes involved with.

Note. It is important that there are clear boundaries between the role of sales and the Bid Manager concerning client negotiations. Unless the Bid Manager happens to be the sales resource as well, the sales negotiations are not the responsibility of the Bid Manager.

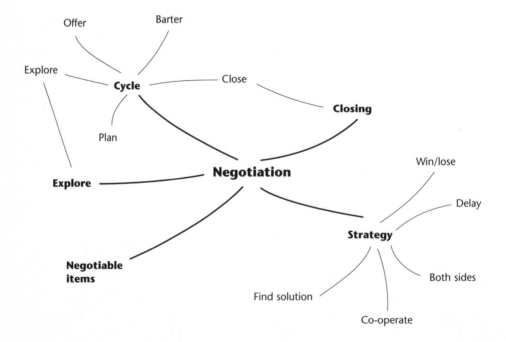

Figure 12.1 *Mind Map®: Negotiation*

This chapter provides a practical guide to the basics of negotiation to help Bid Managers become more effective in gaining access to the resources they need to do the job. The Mind Map® in Figure 12.1 provides an overview of how the chapter fits together.

Negotiation cycle

First of all some theory that describes what actually happens during a negotiation. There is a five-step cycle that can be used to describe the progression of a negotiation. The steps are plan, explore, offer, barter, and close (at which point it starts again, see Figure 12.2).

This list explains what to do during each step, that is, what should be done in order to negotiate effectively.

Step 1 – Plan

There are two parts to this – prioritizing and 'knowing the audience'.

(a) Prioritizing. Before a negotiation is started it is a good idea to know what you want out of it. Make a list of what is required and then put priorities on it. The high-priority items will be the absolute must have ones (for example a printer to produce the bid). The medium ones are important preferences, but not the end of the world (for example someone to edit the bid). The low priority ones are in the would be nice but does not make much difference (for example having a spare desk for visitors to the bid team). The idea is to know what you can happily sacrifice in the negotiating process and what you must fight for. Keep in mind that your priority may not be the same as the other person's. For instance, they may have an editor sitting around doing nothing and, as a consequence, be short of desk space. You get an editor, they get more space; you have traded a low-priority item for a medium one. They have traded a high-priority one for a low one.

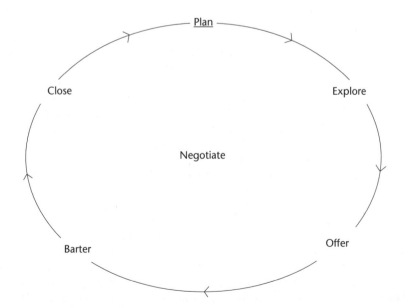

Figure 12.2   *The negotiation cycle*

(b) 'Knowing your audience', in other words, whom are you negotiating with? People's roles make a difference to how they will negotiate and what matters to them. It is important to know if the person/people you are dealing with directly are the ones who will make the decision or is/are influencers of that decision. For example, you may be dealing with the line manager whose staff are sharing the same office space as your bid team. However, the decision on desk allocation may rest with a facilities management group or Human Resources who are based on a separate site. This will influence how you negotiate.

Note: Decision makers sign cheques, agree deals, put their name to the contract, agree the deal. Influencers are their advisers, they are involved in the decision but do not actually take final responsibility for the outcome.

Step 2 – Explore

This is where investing time pays dividends (this is one case where a Bid Manager should not follow the maxim of saving time at all costs). Once you know who you are dealing with and what you want (outputs from Step 1) it is tempting to start negotiating on the spot. Do not do this. Explore the options and talk to the other people involved. Ask open questions, the ones without yes/no answers (for example, 'what are your critical resource issues at the moment?'). You want to find out what they want, show that you understand their priorities and build some degree of rapport if possible. Whilst this progresses, make sure that what is discussed gets summarized, otherwise there is a danger that you will start negotiating for different things.

The purpose of exploratory discussions are to gauge the other's views, create an open dialogue and check your understanding and any preconceptions you may have. It is also a chance to reduce tension and build rapport. In many cases this step takes up to 80 per cent of the time for any negotiation. (See also recipe for discussion later in this chapter.)

Step 3 – Offer

You should not start this step until you can summarize what the other side wants and have a clear understanding of what you want. This is what most people think of as the start of negotiation. Here each side needs to make the starting position clear, stating what they want. You must leave yourself room for manoeuvre here – if you start with the least you will accept, then there is nowhere for you to go. Also, do not mention all the options open to you, the secondary low- and medium-priority items you may throw into the pot later. You want to be able to use the 'if/then' approach where you offer something extra on condition that the other side offers something else. For example, 'If we give up an extra desk space, can we use your photocopier all day on the 27th?'

Step 4 – Barter

Carrying on from offer, this is the real haggling stage and is akin to the street trader offering to throw in a pound of apples if you buy two sacks of potatoes. What you do here is critical. There is a golden rule, 'never give anything away without asking for something in return'. This is 'if/then' again, for example, 'If we give up one day a week of our editor to help out with another bid, can we have a day a week of their technical specialist?' It is useful if you can link items, then they can be bargained off against each other, in this case resource. The author has had considerable success with bartering occasional long hours on site with home-based working – the link being flexibility of labour.

This can all get very complicated, so it as essential that you take notes so that you know where you are. This is doubly important if this stage takes place over more than one meeting – you need to know exactly what was on offer.

Step 5 – Close

The last step. A deal has been struck and there is a definition of what is going to happen. Document this, for internal negotiations an email or a memo will do.

This is necessary because after it is documented both sides can read it and agree that it correctly defines the deal. It also serves as an audit trail to reduce the chances of future disputes over who said/agreed to what. It is vitally important that a full stop should be put on negotiations at this stage if there are any signs that the whole process is about to start up again, so be prepared to stand your ground. (See also separate section later in this chapter.)

The reason the steps are shown forming a circle is that once one deal has been completed the next one can start!

Negotiable items

The following list shows some of the negotiables that a Bid Manager will have to juggle with. These are the resources you need to get the job done and, consequently, the resources you may have to help others with. These are your bargaining counters. The only client negotiables shown relate to the conduct of the bid, not the negotiation of the supply to the client of the end product or service.

Resources – people	This boils down to people's time. The most likely problem will be the time and availability of individuals with specific skills such as technologists, lawyers, accountants or staff whose time is at a premium such as senior managers, operational staff and so on. There will also be calls upon the bid team to provide their services to others, so it will not always require a negotiation to obtain resource, but to keep it. Of course this presents an opportunity for bargaining.
Resources – space and equipment	Bids tend to be one-off events (even in organizations that do comparatively large numbers of them), so there are unlikely to be dedicated facilities to support them. Even in organizations that do have some bid specific facilities there will be competition for them. The normal situation is that most of the facilities required will need to be set up from scratch. This means that desks, phones, computer equipment, network access, meeting rooms and so forth will be potential negotiable items. As with people there will be opportunities to negotiate the supply of these resources to other bid teams, sales support and so forth – a potential two-way trade.
Time	Time is always at a premium in any bid. There will be occasions when it is necessary to negotiate with the client for an extension to the timetable for procurement.
Budget	For most Bid Managers the budget will not normally be a major issue. If there is a proper bid approval process, this should include any funding that needs to be accounted for. There will be times when there is a need to purchase capital equipment, for example a high-capacity colour printer that may require special approval.
Client resource/sites	Access to client staff is always an issue. These people usually have a 'real' job to do and have to provide information to bidders in addition to this. Similarly, any site visits need to be organized so as not to impact existing operations. As this will be done in competition to the other bidders, there will always be pressure on client resources. Consequently, it will often be necessary to negotiate access.
Priorities	At first sight this seems somewhat abstract in comparison to the 'real' items

above. But, the priorities people have to getting something done, how important office space is, value of a piece of equipment and so on vary considerably. What may be a high priority to one side of a negotiation may not be to the other.

> *Note.* It is often difficult to negotiate from a position of strength as a Bid Manager. The problem is that the Bid Managers are invariably asking others to provide them with resources, but have none directly under their own control. Consequently, they are seldom in a position to offer that much in return. However, they are often going to be running bids in the future, or have done in the past, that directly affect the bottom line for the resource holders. Also, by communicating well and keeping people up to date, a balance of credibility will accrue. Trade on this.

Negotiation strategies

These strategies are well established and cover most situations. Those who have read the conflict-handling section in Chapter 10 will have come across the basic concepts already. The four principle strategies are win/lose, delay, look at both sides, solve the problem and co-operate.

WIN/LOSE

This is a primitive strategy where one party aims to win at all costs, irrespective of the impact and expense to the other side. In practice win/lose can only work where there is an absolute point that cannot be negotiated or there is no intention of ever working with the other side again. Within a bid, an example of a non-negotiable might be provision of a printer to print the bid on. Without one there would be no bid. It is somewhat unlikely that such a situation would occur. It is even harder to think of an example where there would be no desire to work with the other party again – the people being negotiated with work for the same organization.

Where might this approach be appropriate in a bid? In the author's experience there are relatively few opportunities when this will be beneficial. It may be useful in a negotiation with an incumbent supplier that is also a competitor. For example, there may be a legal duty for an incumbent supplier to provide information to any competing bidder as part of a due diligence exercise. (Due diligence is the process of ensuring that all people bidding for/making a purchase are entitled to ask, and have answered, all reasonable questions concerning material facts affecting the contract.) It may be beneficial to force them to supply information, or make them look inefficient because they cannot supply it in time, in this case taking a win/lose strategy by refusing to compromise on what is delivered or the timetable.

DELAY

Although not as negative a method as win/lose the opportunity to use delay as a tactic is limited by the speed of events within a typical bid. Here the strategy is to put off the negotiation to a future date in the hope that things may be more favourable then. The problem with this is that it can only be used when it does not matter if there is a delay before matters are concluded. For example, it might be acceptable to have a delay of a few days before someone was made available to take on the role of editor for the bid in the early stages, in which case negotiating for this resource could be left for a while. However, when this strategy is adopted it is important to set a timetable for when the negotiation must be resumed.

LOOK AT BOTH SIDES

This is closely related to the 'explore' stage of the negotiation cycle. The principal is to understand both sides of the deal and make sure that the key points are summarized. This allows both sides to agree what their relative positions are. It is worth applying this method at any stage in the negotiation when there seems to be a misunderstanding. Looking at both sides is more of a technique than a negotiation strategy because it gathers information rather than makes an offer to be haggled over. It is only part of the overall strategy.

CO-OPERATION

The starting point for co-operation is having a common understanding of each other's situation and respecting that viewpoint. It is a very good point to start a negotiation from as not only will it mean that there is a common understanding but also that there is a basis for fair bargaining. Essentially you are showing that you will accommodate their needs whilst trying to fulfil your own. As with looking at both sides this is only part of the story, you are not actually negotiating but establishing the basis for the negotiation.

FIND A SOLUTION – THE WIN/WIN DEAL

In an ideal world this has to be the best strategy (unfortunately, few bids take place in an entirely ideal world). The basis is in agreeing to work together to find a joint solution to the problem to be solved – completing the negotiation. For example, consider the case where the issue is office space and staff resource where the bid is competing with another department's activities. Obviously it would be possible to put forward a case for why you and not they should have the resource. You may well win if the bid is important enough. This would smack of win/lose. However, if the Bid Manager got together with the appropriate department head and agreed to work towards a solution based upon resource sharing, pooling space and equipment and so on, there could be significant benefits to both sides. It is quite possible that there will be benefits from 'synergy' in the form of shared knowledge, or access to better equipment that might not otherwise have been available even in a co-operative approach.

SUMMARY

It will be necessary to use all these strategies from time to time. However, the most effective will be the win/win solution. The benefits of this were given above but, in addition, the collaborative nature of this strategy will have benefits in the attitude of the organization to the client. If people feel that they have lost out in terms of their trading with the bid team they can easily transfer this attitude to the client once the business has been won. The consequence of this can be very significant in the longer term and can result in unhappy client and lost business.

Exploring within a discussion

Because the 'Explore' step can take up to 80 per cent of the time in a negotiation the following recipe is offered, together with dos and don'ts to help the novice Bid Manager through any negotiations. See also the section on meetings in Chapter 11.

RECIPE

This is valid for almost any meeting, but is particularly useful for discussions leading up to negotiations:

Create rapport	Before the discussion gets going make sure everyone knows everyone else, what they do and where the come from. Ice-breaking topics such as the weather, travel problems can help, as can the social interaction of getting coffee. This is basically the 'small talk' session where you get comfortable with each other. *Don't miss this out* – getting down to business immediately may save time, but it does not put you, or the rest of the meeting, at ease. If done well, it is the start of a successful relationship. If people already know each other well then this will not be such an issue, but this part of 'meeting and greeting' is important in any negotiation.
Set the agenda	This must be done co-operatively. Agree an agenda for the discussion that meets the needs of all involved. It gives a structure to hang the discussions upon.
Define scope	Set the scope and the limits for the negotiation, what will and will not be discussed.
Ask open questions	Avoid questions with yes/no answers (such as 'do you want more desk space'). Open questions such as, 'What sort of staff resources issues do you currently have?' promote discussion and increase the chances of soliciting useful information.
Listen positively	Do not interrupt. Maintain appropriate levels of eye contract and nod to show you have understood a point.
Look for signals	Keep a lookout for verbal and visual cues that indicate a response to an idea. This will help identify what is important, or what is boring. For example, folded arms and wandering attention, looking out the window and so on are evidence of boredom and possible irritation. Strong eye contact, nodding and encouraging questions, and general increases in activity show that the current topic matters.
Summarize	When a particular agenda item or a discrete topic within a discussion is concluded, summarize what has been said and make sure that everyone agrees that it is an accurate summary.
Adjourn	Do not try and negotiate until everyone has had time to digest the information that they have gained from the discussion. Once each side has a good idea of what the other wants then positive offers can be made.

DOS AND DON'TS

Do	Don't
Listen to what the other side has to say.	*Interrupt* when the other party is giving you information.
Clarify with questions to make sure that you have understood the information given to you.	*Threaten*.
Respond positively to collaboration and information giving.	*Respond to intransigence*, do not let yourself get pulled into a row.
Summarize what has been said – it helps clarify what was said, and meant.	*Forget to summarize* what has been said. This is another chance to check understanding.
Seek information, you need to know what the other party wants, when they want it, where and why. If you do not know this you will find it hard to understand what they will find attractive as an offer or a concession.	*Talk too much* as it can prevent the other side from giving you useful information and may make them feel they haven't been allowed to state their position.
Be non-committal, do not make any premature deals whilst you are still gathering information. You may well find that you have given away something you did not need to or have undervalued something that did not seem useful at the time that could have gained you a better deal later.	*Argue to win*, as even when you do it will only harden attitudes and create an uncooperative atmosphere (see above on intransigence)
Give information, you need to make sure that the other side has a good understanding of what you want, and why you want it, when and where.	*Show your hand*, in particular do not let them work out what your bottom line is or what you have kept in hand for further negotiation.
Make notes, you will need them later, it may be useful to have minutes but it will certainly be essential to know what was said.	*Forget to take notes*, you really will need them later.

Closing a negotiation

As with discussion, this step in the negotiation cycle is sufficiently important to be worth expanding on and possible closing techniques and some dos and don'ts are offered to help with this critical stage.

STRATEGIES

There are five basic closing techniques that are considered: summary close, final offer close, thinking time close, options close and ultimatum close. Simple examples are given to help a Bid Manager choose the one that might be appropriate at the time:

Summary	The method is to draw all the facts and figures together and summarize what you have conceded. Then highlight the benefits to the other party of these concessions. Finally, call for agreement on what you have proposed. The deal is now done.
	You might say, 'We've agreed to give up two desk spaces in the main office and share the use of our microwave. This means that all your team can now sit together and they won't have to go next door to heat up their lunch. So you

	will get improved productivity from better team communications and a reduction in wasted time going for lunch. So can we agree that my team has exclusive use of the small office as a bid room?'
Final offer	Make a final offer to clinch the deal (make this too big and they will think there is more to come; too little and it will seem silly). Note that you cannot go further than a final offer, once you have made that you have burned your boats. If this strategy does not work, then you have no deal. This is the risk associated with this strategy and the wise Bid Manager will only adopt it when no deal is an acceptable outcome.
Thinking time	This is useful if things seem to be at a stalemate. Summarize your offer and suggest a specified thinking time break. Each party then goes away and thinks about it before returning for a re-match. However, before going away agreement must be made on time and place for the return meeting. If an urgent decision is needed, or the matter is really pressing, this may not be practical. For example, towards the end of a bid when time is short this may not be an available option.
Options	Make an 'either/or' offer and ask the other party to choose what they want. This is a classic closing strategy and is sometimes called the 'Do you want it in red or blue?' close. Obviously you need to have options to offer.
	For instance, 'If we can have access to your high-performance colour printer for two days a week, you can either put it on my desk or have it in our bid room'.
Ultimatum	The approach is to summarize and call for a decision by a certain time. Then point out the consequences of not making a decision by that time. For example, 'We need the approval to continue with the bid by Friday in order to meet the client's timetable. Without that decision we will not be able to bid at all'. This is an even more risky strategy than the 'final offer' one. So, be very careful with this as it can close down a negotiation without a conclusion. It raises the stakes on any deal and should be used only if a negative outcome is acceptable.

DOS AND DON'TS OF CLOSING

As with most human interactions there are some things that help and some things that hinder during the closing step of a negotiation. These Dos and Don'ts are based upon experience and research:

Do	Don't
Decide when to stop, do not risk opening things up again.	*Go on too long*, because you will open things up again!
Write down what is agreed, if you do not then the deal is not really closed, it is a matter of opinion.	*Get euphoric*, it is too easy to get carried away and start offering new goodies whilst under the influence of an excess of goodwill.
Bluff with your final offer.	*Make closing concessions*.
Clarify all agreements, it is important that all parties properly understand the deal. Even when it is written down, if people did not understand it they may try and go back on it. Worse, they may feel that they have been deliberately misled.	*Use loose definitions* as it makes it hard to know what the actual deal is and it won't stick.
Make benefit statements that show how everyone wins from the deal. Make sure these are clearly understood.	*Dither*, a decision has to be made one way or the other.

Stick to your finish position. Once the deal is made do not restart the negotiation again.

End on a win/win note, as it is important that the deal is seen to be good for all concerned. This will help cement the agreement and have a beneficial carry on for future negotiations.

Look forward to the next deal.

Cheat, you will get found out and then you will not be trusted to deal again.

Disclose your real bottom line. If you do then you either leave the other side feeling cheated if you have agreed on more, or leave yourself with nowhere to go.

Lose your objective. There was a reason you went into this negotiation; do not forget it in the thrill of the deal.

CASE STUDY

SITUATION

NB, a multinational supplier, was bidding to manage the property portfolio of BS Investment. This was to include everything from cleaning the buildings and security through catering to the maintenance of high-technology infrastructure and telecommunications. BS Investment had over 50 properties spread out over three countries. They currently obtained these services from five different suppliers, some of whom would be bidding for the new contract. The goal was to save money by only having to deal with a single organization and so obtain a better overall deal. The timetable for the procurement was very short, the intention being to have the new supplier in place before the start of the next financial year. This decision was taken without any real assessment of the size of the task involved. BS Investment had not run such a complex procurement before.

PROBLEM

The timetable for the bid had not been set with any understanding of how long the job would actually take. It was clear to the Bid Manager and the sales manager that NB were not going to be able to complete the response within the timetable given by BS Investment. They suspected that their competitors would also be having a major problem with this too. An internal SWOT meeting was held and it was agreed that they would be unable to put forward a worthwhile bid within the timescale. The lack of information available combined with the time

would inevitably mean that very conservative assumptions would have to be made forcing the adoption of an uncompetitive pricing model. It was also felt that those organizations that did have staff on site already had an advantage in this respect. This was seen as a real threat to winning the business.

ACTION TAKEN

As there was felt to be little or no chance of winning on the existing timetable it was decided to go back to the client with the following offer: to ask for a two week extension for the bid during which time NB staff would meet with BS staff to collate the due diligence information that would be needed. In case this might be seen as an unfair tactic by competitors NB offered to share all the basic data gathered and to agree to competitor staff being present at on-site meetings if they wished. This offer was to be made because NB knew that BS did not have staff available internally to complete this exercise without help and that they did not have time to get in independent consultants without completely losing sight of the timetable. From the client's point of view this might not be ideal, but it would get them out of a hole. If they accepted it would also indicate that they were keen for NB to bid and that they were considered a credible supplier. The plan was simply to ask for the extension and offer the assistance only if BS suggested that they would not be able to do the job in the time. The 'free' consultancy was not going to be part of the initial proposition.

OUTCOME

NB approached the procurement manager at BS with the proposition as described. BS acknowledged that at least 'one' of the competitors had also asked for a two-week extension, and that they appreciated the problem. BS had an issue that they simply did not have the staff available to do the work in less than four to five weeks. They were also concerned that they were using some of the competitors' (who were incumbents) staff to gather information. At this point the offer of free consultancy was offered on the basis that, if you were to accept this and agree that distribution of the information made it fair, then NB would be able to bid within two weeks, just about keeping the procurement on track.

LESSON LEARNT

By offering BS what boiled down to 'free' consultancy, NB were able to extend the timetable for the bid without making it look as though they were unable to hit deadlines. They were also able to use the time on site to their advantage by showing how professional their staff were. Furthermore, they demonstrated that they had a real understanding of the portfolio of services that BS would need to manage their property effectively. This more than compensated for any information that would be given out to the competitors and the cost of the staff involved. BS went on to win the business, but only after substantial negotiations on price. This represented a battle won, not the war.

Checklist

Item	Description	Completed?
Negotiable items	Do you know what they are? Yours? Other sides? Have they been prioritized?	
Discussion	Create rapport. Set an agenda. Describe the scope of what you seek. Ask open questions. Listen positively. Look for signals. Summarize both sides' position. Adjourn.	
Negotiation strategy	What is you overall strategy? Win/lose? Delay? Look at both sides? Co-operate? Find a solution?	
Closing strategy	Have you chosen the strategy you intend to use? Summary? Final offer? Thinking time? Options? Ultimatum?	

13 *Sales*

A well-informed employee is the best sales person a company can have. (Edgar Watson Howe)

The goal of this chapter is to help Bid Managers support the sales process, not turn Bid Managers into sales people. The intended audience is people from a non-sales background who end up managing bids. However, even experienced sales staff may find some of the methods described useful. Sales awareness is promoted so that sales driven events are better understood. Methods are put forward that will help the bid team support the sale more effectively (Figure 13.1).

Sales awareness

Being sales aware is a quality that every Bid Manager needs to have, but what does that mean? Simply understanding that objective of the exercise is to win the, hopefully profitable, new business against the competition. This means that the events affecting a bid

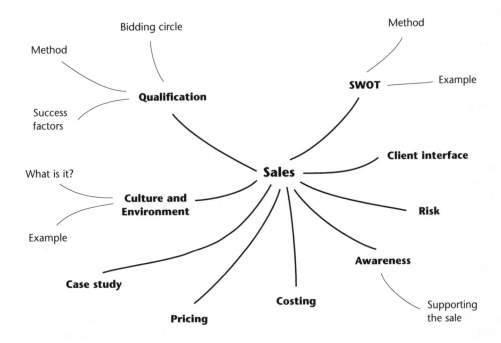

Figure 13.1 *Mind Map®: Sales*

are driven by factors that are not always helpful in terms of the efficient production of bid documents. It also means that what the clients asks for, they get. The conventional project management concept, that there is a specification with a budget attached and some notion of change control, does not apply. This can be difficult for those from a project management or service delivery background to take on board.

> *Key point.* Any bid documents submitted to a client are there to document the concepts that have already been sold to that client. This selling activity will be going on in parallel to the bid production activities. Expect changes in strategy and direction to come from the interaction of sales people with the client.

Those responsible for the sales campaign will be trying to influence the client in many ways. This influence will extend beyond the confines of the particular bid. For example, with an existing client the organization should not be surprised when a bid starts – the sales staff should know about it from their contacts with the client. Indeed, sales staff with a successful relationship with a client will have influenced what the client will ask for, before any bid requests get issued.

The unique selling point (sometimes Proposition – USP) is the Holy Grail of all sales staff. Bid Managers need to be aware that whilst this is a desirable thing, in the real world USPs are few and far between. It is unlikely that one organization can deliver something that no one else can. However, it may well be that the overall package can be put together in such a way that the case for awarding the business to you is hard to ignore. Bid Managers can help by keeping the focus of the bid team on identifying and communicating benefits to the client via both the bid documents and the sales team. The specialists within the bid team will be aware of many things that can benefit the client that are not apparent to a non-specialist sales person. Recognizing this is part of sales awareness.

> *Note.* Change and the ability to adapt to change is the natural consequence of working in a customer/sales-driven world. All bids take place in that world.

SUPPORTING THE SALE

There are many things a Bid Manager can do to support the sale. Being sales aware is a start because it enables the Bid Manager to understand why things are happening. At a more practical level there are tools and methods that can be used to support the sales campaign. Examples of these are provided in the remaining sections of this chapter and the reader is encouraged to adopt a positive attitude to finding ways that improve the chances of winning the bid.

Risk register as a sales tool

As discussed in Chapter 4, clients can, and do, ask for a risk register and/or plan that indicates the client's view of the products and services being supplied. This presents the supplier with both an opportunity and a liability. For example, if your organization can supply all the client needs 'in house' then there is obviously a lower risk associated with this than there is with a competitor that needs to use several subcontractors. You might choose to include the following risk in your register:

Risk ID	Description	Impact	Prob.	Contingency plan/owner	Date
4	Managing multiple subcontractors increases chances of problems in supply chain.	H	L	Supplier organization has all necessary elements of the supply chain within its own group of companies.	14/6/04

This entry obviously makes the point to anyone who inspects the register. Keep in mind that the competitors may well be doing this to expose the weaknesses they perceive your organization to have.

> *Note.* Any risk that you put in a risk register you give to a supplier needs to be justifiable. It is a dubious practice, and a high-risk one, to try and undermine the opposition with false risks. You will be found out, and the consequences can extend far further than just losing the sale.

SWOT analysis

There are a whole host of different sales and sales support techniques and tools that are available today. However, there is one in particular that the author has found to be very useful in supporting a bid – SWOT, which stands for strengths, weaknesses, opportunities and threats.

METHOD

An example is provided in the next section that will expand upon this, but the recipe here provides a six-step approach:

Evaluation criteria	To provide focus decide what are the areas that you wish to consider for the analysis, for example price, ability to deliver, track record and so on.
Brainstorming meeting	Identify the strengths and weaknesses without any attempt at analysis. It does not matter if you get the same ones in different words. Next identify which are the unique strengths/weaknesses and remove the duplicates. *For instance, a long-term relationship with the client might be a strength, a history of letting that client down would be a weakness.*
Competition	If possible, measure up the competition against the identified key strengths and weaknesses. This will be based upon the knowledge of the team of the competition – this will be less accurate than knowledge of your own company, though possibly less subjective.
Opportunities	What opportunities present themselves either for yourself or to the disadvantage of the competition. Identify where you can capitalize on the strengths. *For example, a competitor may not have the ability to deliver required equipment without a subcontractor – you can do so directly. You would make it clear to the client what the benefits of a single source of supply were.*
Threats	Determine where weaknesses can be mitigated.
Action	Agree on the actions to be taken in order to benefit from the opportunities and threats above.

SWOT example

This example is based upon a number of real SWOT exercises that the author was involved with. Minor changes have been made for reasons of confidentiality. It concerns the long list to shortlist stage of procurement for a service supply contract. BS are bidding for the renewal of this contract, but with added services and new customer requirements. The new contract was also to run for a longer time than the original. BS were doing a reasonable job as sitting tenants, but were by no means everyone's favourite and had made some significant errors. The example shows how a SWOT exercise was used to decide the tactics to be used when bidding to get on the shortlist.

> *Note.* Purists will point out that what is described here is not a textbook SWOT. This does not matter, the reality is that an analysis was made based upon strengths and weaknesses that led to a decision on how to progress the bid. Be pragmatic about methods and tailor them to your needs.

EVALUATION CRITERIA

These had been identified and were used to provide a focus for the SWOT meeting:

- Value for money: not necessarily the cheapest solution, but one where the costs are outweighed by the benefits.
- Confidence in the supplier.
- Complete range of services: must be able to get everything from the supplier.
- Innovation: looking for newer and better ways of getting what they have, plus more.
- Ability of the supplier to partner at the business level as well as provide services.
- Seamless service supply: the client sees no boundaries where one service stops and another one starts.

STRENGTHS AND WEAKNESSES

With these in mind a brainstorming session was held (see Chapter 11 on communications for advice on running such meetings) to identify BS's strengths and weaknesses. These were written on a whiteboard without any attempt to analyse them (for example removing duplicates). Those present at the meeting included sales, sales management, technical specialists, the manager of current services supplied to the client, the Bid Manager, departmental managers and so on, about 12 people in all. This was a large group and a facilitator/scribe was essential to make this work. See the section on meetings in Chapter 10 for guidance on facilitation.

Strengths

1 Partnership with critical component supplier	14 Can show ability to offer new solution *before* contract award
2 Can accommodate change	15 BS capability (near total) to do everything needed
3 Wide market sector knowledge/track record	16 Breadth of service
4 Wide skill set	17 Track record of innovation

5   BS know customer
6   Low risk/fear of change
7   Track record
8   Relationships with key people
9   'Already there'
10 Knowledge of infrastructure
11 Cost of transition
12 Client market knowledge
13 Understand the business

18 Quality company
19 BS management commitment to bid
20 On-site presence (sitting tenant)
21 Partner management
22 Scale of change achieved to date
23 'Don't give up' on projects
24 Impartiality
25 Client staff support (they like BS)

Weaknesses

1   Cannot meet business consultancy requirement
2   Lack of consistent people/contacts
3   Don't communicate deliverables – surprises
4   'Hidden agenda' – what does the client's MD want?
5   Are we lowest cost?
6   Not proactive
7   Multiple points of contact (both sales and delivery)
8   Different departments within BS seen as fragmented
9   Helpdesk – skills/resource too low
10 Helpdesk perceived as unresponsive
11 Current contract constraints

12 No consultancy skills in house (partners?)
13 Not perceived as innovative
14 Not profitable
15 Reactive management style
16 Senior BS management support lacking
17 Track record, e.g. poor service record
18 Over a year to deliver against previous procurement
19 Not perceived as partner but as supplier

20 Failure to communicate successes
21 Follow-up on detail

OPPORTUNITY AND THREAT ANALYSIS

It is at this point that a break was made from the classical approach to SWOT. Instead of looking at opportunities and threats as such, a discussion was held to map these strengths and weaknesses onto categories that the competition should be scored upon. Effectively this combined the opportunities with the threats by looking at where the competition was strong/weak.

Based upon the strengths and weaknesses identified, specific categories were chosen upon which to score BS and the competition. The list below specifies them and shows *some* examples of how they mapped on to the brainstorming session.

Category	Description	Strength	Weakness
Client relationship and history	Relationship with the client and history of previous work done for the client.		17, 19, 20
Market sector	Experience within the client's particular market sector.		
Management of service	Quality of the organization as a supplier of a managed service.		3, 9, 10
Systems supply	Ability to supply equipment and its installation.		
Consultancy	Ability to provide management consultancy to the client at high level.		1, 12
Support skill level	Organization's depth of support knowledge and how many people with relevant skills are available to support client.	10, 20	

Catering/facilities	Ability to operate catering and accommodation services to the client sites.

The competitors who had bid at the long-list stage were identified as BS themselves plus MBA, ANO, NB, BAD, HAL, XYZ and BSC. *Note*: these company acronyms are all fictitious. The team that was involved in the brainstorming for the strengths and weaknesses made their estimates for each of the competitors based upon knowledge and 'gut feel'. The quality of this exercise would vary according to the level of knowledge available to the team. In this case some of the team had worked for, or with, many of the competitor companies.

Category/Competitor	BS	MBA	ANO	NB	BAD	HAL	XYZ	BSC
Client history/relationship	5	4	0	0	0	3	2	4
Market sector	4	4	2	3	0	4	4	4
Management of service	5	0	2	0	0	3	5	4
Systems supply	5	5	5	3	2	5	5	4
Consultancy	0	4	5	5	0	5	3	1
Support skill	5	0	0	0	0	2	5	1
Catering/facilties	3	2	2	0	0	5	4	2
Total	27	19	16	11	2	27	28	20

It was clear from these esitmates that BS, HAL and XYZ were the main contenders, with BSC and MBA as possible contenders. It was also clear that BAD were only there as a potential system supplier. However, looking at the distribution of the scores suggested that the shortlist might have been created with the intention of encouraging suppliers to link up to form partnerships.

Given the consultancy 'gap' in the BS offering it seemed that MBA, ANO, NB and HAL were the best matches. However, MBA and HAL were such strong contenders that it was unlikely they would want to partner. Also, as they were competitors across the board, it would be difficult to decide who would supply what – there was no niche to fit in with. This left ANO and NB the best fit to plug the consultancy gap in the BS offering.

The sales manager revealed that NB had already approached BS with a view to a deal. This would be a high-scoring partnership and would give a higher score than any competitor. It would also have the benefit of eliminating one competitor (as they would now be a partner) and removing the opportunity for one of the other high scorers to partner with them. ANO could be kept in reserve in case no deal could be made with NB.

In SWOT terms the 'opportunity' was to choose a partner, the 'threats' were the competitors.

A decision was made to form a partnership with NB with a view to a joint bid, and this was indeed what was done. The result was that the joint bid was successful in getting on the shortlist. The SWOT session had been a key factor in identifying that this was the best way forward.

Sales themes and the bid brief

Sales themes, the underlying messages of a bid, can be a significant contributor to the success of a sales campaign. These are simple messages, for example 'saving you time', that run through the entire bid. Identifying these is something that the Bid Manager can drive as part of the job.

The use of a bid brief as a planning, communication and control aid has been well documented in other chapters (3, 5 and 6). It is also a good vehicle for keeping track of sales themes for the bid. First, sales themes need to be identified and this is a task that can be facilitated by the Bid Manager. A good way to do this is to adopt a similar approach to the SWOT example given earlier.

Start by gathering together the members of the bid team, and any others relevant to the task, into a brainstorming meeting. Follow the non-analytic/non-critical approach for the first stage as usual and then distil the key sales themes from this. These themes need to be documented, preferably in the bid brief, and then circulated to those writing the bid.

It can be helpful to develop this further and identify sub-themes that support the main ones that can then be incorporated into individual, possibly specialist, areas of the bid. For example, ability to deliver a complete information technology service might have sub-themes in such areas as training, technology updates and maintenance and repair. Communicating this to the team will enable them to put together a consistent bid.

Client interaction

The Bid Manager is often the prime point of contact with the client. However, the client often sees the role as being less sales oriented than that of any sales staff working on the bid. This presents the Bid Manager with the opportunity to gain information whilst performing what are notionally administrative functions. For example, it is reasonable to ask how the bid is going when submitting questions about the bid. The client may let slip that they are ahead of/behind schedule. Such information can open up opportunities for sales to, in this case, offer help, or perhaps suggest an extension to the timetable (if beneficial). The Bid Manager may not be directly fulfilling a sales role, but will have many chances to help the sale along.

Qualifying the client/bid

This is an area where the Bid Manager can support the sales organization with the sale and also support the organization in the effective use of resources.

THE BIDDING CIRCLE

There is a vicious circle that occurs in bids that is worth mentioning because it is so common. It goes something like this. There is an advert in a journal for a procurement that is potentially worth a significant sum to your organization. It is only a few days' work to respond to the initial questionnaire asking about your company and its financial stability, number of staff, relevant expertise and so forth. So you do this as it has little impact on the business. This is successful and you get put on a long list of a dozen or so suppliers. However, to respond to the request for information that is sent out to the long-list potential suppliers is more work. But, the client has shown interest so there must be a good chance of getting the business. A bid team is formed and considerable time and effort is spent. Again, you make it to the next stage, a shortlist of three and an invitation to tender. At this point it is noticed that the other two companies on the shortlist both have an existing relationship with the client. What is more the services required are more in their line than yours. Do you still bid? Well, you have spent a considerable amount of money getting this far and it is a sales opportunity that is worth chasing, so you go for it. More money is spent and you come in an honourable second. The old saying, throwing good money after bad springs to mind. Somewhere along the line the argument switched from, 'it doesn't cost too much', to, 'look how much we've spent, it won't cost us that much more to carry on'. Has this ever happened in your organization? It is the author's experience that it is very hard to stop a bid once it has started. It is so rare that every time it has happened is memorable!

A BETTER WAY

There is a very simple solution to this problem, qualification. Unfortunately, it is very hard to put in place and even harder to keep in place (and, even where it has proved itself over many years, a takeover or merger will often remove it). But that does not mean organizations should not try it. If you look at the costs of running major bids and then look at the success rate, it rapidly becomes clear that there is scope for saving money, and spending it on better things.

There are real benefits from only bidding for business that you are likely to win (based upon more than just a sales person's instinct):

- Resources are focused where they will produce results.
- Cost of sale is reduced improving overall profitability.
- Chances of winning are increased, improving market share.
- Quality of delivered bids increases making the organization appear more professional.
- Staff morale is increased because they are involved in more successful bids.

Some organizations have established qualification processes either as part of their project management or sales methodologies. The goal of these is to have an established set of criteria against which a bid is measured so that a go/no go decision can be made in a rational manner. The author is aware of one company that was very successful with such a method because they made the default decision a negative one. The sales/bid team had to make a very strong case or no resources would be provided to run the bid. This resulted in a surprisingly high 'hit rate' for this organization.

> *Note.* Saying 'no' to a bid can be used as a qualification technique itself – if the client really wants your organization it will make this very clear and encourage you to change your mind. This puts you in a strong position.

QUALIFICATION METHOD

What follows is a recipe for producing a bid qualification process. Such a process will be highly dependent on the culture and structure of the organization concerned and its implementation will be beyond the authority of most Bid Managers. However, if such a method is to work then the Bid Manager will need to provide support for much of the process. Five components will be needed to make up a simple qualification process:

Criteria/thresholds	For the specified criteria some thresholds will need to be identified that determine who will approve the bid and form the basis upon which the decision will be made. These will normally include some or all of:

Value of business in turnover;
Profitability of business;
Risk (financial, technical, market presence, client relationship);
Probability of winning;
Resources required;
Cost of sale;
Market specific;
Client specific.

Decision makers	Depending on the value/risk/chance of winning (or other criteria) there will need to be a person/set of people who make the bid/no bid decision. These will typically be drawn from:

Sales management;
Finance;
Legal;
Marketing;
Human resources;
Operational and delivery management.

Decision points	Depending on how the organization operates, the size of the bid and so on, there needs to be a forum where the decision makers meet at specific points during the life of a bid.
Documentation	There needs to be some sort of documentation to support the scoring of the criteria and to provide the raw material for the decision makers to study. Ideally this should be made up of the documentation that has been produced to support the bid in the first place.
Presentation	A short presentation should be given to the decision makers, possibly by the sales person, with critical members of the bid team available to answer questions. Suggested agenda:

Overview of sale;
Key success factors;
Evaluation against the criteria;
Resource requirement to bid.

QUALIFICATION SUCCESS FACTORS

When putting together the process that defines how all these things are fitted together it is a good idea to make it as non-bureaucratic as possible. Also make the amount of non-bid/sales related work a minimum. Sales people and bid teams will not support any process which they think takes too much time away from the work for the client.

The following will help:

- Use a simple form to fill in for the criteria/risk.
- Have a standard agenda for the presentation/decision-making meeting.
- Use existing bid documents (such as bid brief) to support presentations.
- Keep documentation to a minimum – minute actions/decisions only.

- Train, and retrain people in what to do.
- Promote the benefits (resource availability, higher hit rates, and bigger profits) often.

All the above are necessary if the process is going to survive and deliver real benefits.

Culture and environment

Although this is not skill related in the way that the other chapters in Part 3 are, the effect of the culture of both the client and the supplier organizations is often very significant. There is little the Bid Manager can do to change these cultures, but awareness of their importance is vital.

WHAT IS MEANT BY CULTURE?

Culture refers to the way people behave, the way things get done and the 'traditions' within an organization. It is affected by gender, religion, education, personal circumstances, history, politics, geography and so on.

To see examples of this, compare and contrast the way a military unit and an advertising company might operate on a day-to-day basis. One would be hierarchical, disciplined and highly organized, and formally attired, the other would be informal, more random, casually dressed and, possibly, more creative. Both are suited to the tasks they carry out, but if they had to work together the cultural differences would be very apparent. So, it is reasonable to expect cultural differences by occupation/market. However, these differences also exist within industries, across national boundaries, societies and so forth. For example, the founders of a small company that then grows into a large one can have a profound impact on the behavioural norms of the organization.

EXAMPLE

This short case study highlights the type of problem that culture clashes can cause. It is by no means an extreme condition and is loosely based on the author's own experience. In many cases it will not be an issue, if you are bidding within your own market area then the culture of the organizations tend not to be too different. However, when bidding across international, market sector and similar major boundaries then cultural issues can, and do, grow into major problems.

CASE STUDY

SITUATION

BS plc was bidding for a property services contract for a national retail consortium. This required a broad range of services including building maintenance and refurbishment, utilities management, security services and the provision of the information technology infrastructure. BS plc had all these services available in house, with the exception of IT. As this bid was to one of their existing clients, indeed a major client, they did not want to lose it and consequently went in search of a suitable company to act as a subcontractor. Based on the recommendation of their internal IT organization they went to XYZcom, who were known to be market leaders in the relevant area. XYZcom seemed a safe and attractive option as they were already supporting similar infrastructures in other retail companies. Max F was the sales manager for the project and his background in civil engineering and property services meant that he had both sales and management skills that combined with industry knowledge to make him the natural choice to manage the bid.

PROBLEM

Initially all seemed to go well; BS plc was well versed in the production of such bids and Max F was an old hand at the job. In the early stages all that was required from XYZcom was a statement of competence and descriptions of reference sites where they had done similar work. There was relatively little interaction between those working on the bid at BS and XYZcom. However, once it was established that BS and one other company were now the favourites to win the business it became clear that the competition was going to be tough. In particular, it appeared that the client had a major problem with its existing IT infrastructure and that it saw the resolution of this as critical. Getting this right would be essential if BS were to win the business. Consequently, Max decided to increase the involvement of XYZcom in the bid, treating them more like a partner than a subcontractor. They were to take a very visible role from now on.

Unfortunately, the cultures of the two organizations were very different. On the one hand, BS plc was very formal in the way it did things, having a background in civil engineering project management as a core strength.

On the other hand, XYZcom tended to follow an ad hoc approach to meetings and design. One of its key strengths was the ability to react quickly to changing situations. It was not unusual for a meeting around the coffee machine to result in a completely different solution to the one that had existed first thing in the morning.

It was in meetings that the culture clash was at its greatest. BS plc meetings followed a strict agenda – if it was not on the agenda then a separate meeting would be set up to deal with it. XYZcom staff would go off at tangents and would often not get past item one on the agenda because they had held the equivalent of two completely different meetings and had overrun by an hour before item two. Both these approaches have their strengths and weaknesses and each can be very effective in the right environment. The real problem was that they did not combine. The people at the meetings were driving each other mad and rancour was setting in with a vengeance.

OUTCOME

The bid was completed successfully, however the relationship between the XYZcom and BS was now very poor. During the latter stages of the bid interaction between the two companies was done at arms length. Exchange of information took place by email only.

LESSON LEARNT

The cultures of the two companies were very different and conflicts were inevitable. The Bid Manager needs to act to head them off before they damage the effectiveness of the bid team. This means being aware of culture and corporate attitudes, and being prepared to accommodate them.

> *Hint.* Whenever you are dealing with a client that is new to you, it is always a good idea to have a look at their website on the Internet. As well as being a valuable source of information, it will also give you clue as to their culture. If their website looks jazzy and has jokes and cartoons, it will suggest less formality than one that just provides a copy of the latest annual report. Also there is a considerable amount of information to be gained from some of these web sites that can help with the bid.

Costing

This is another area where the Bid Manager can help the sales process. Unless the bid is very simple, in which case you probably will not be reading this book, the costing of the bid will be a major activity in itself. It will inevitably involve the use of a spreadsheet, and collating costs from a variety of sources. This should be built into the plan for the bid, at least to the level of who is responsible for delivering the cost information.

Costs can usefully be split into either one-off or recurrent categories. Some examples are:

One-off	Set-up costs – purchase of premises/fixed assets, cost of the bid itself.
(Start-up)	Initial training and familiarization.
	Document creation.
	Staff take on (plus TUPE – see Glossary).
	One-off equipment/maintenance upgrades.
	Replacement of defective equipment.
	Stock take on at valuation.
	Legal fees.
	Development costs.
Recurrent	Staff.
(operating costs)	Consumables.
	Upgrades to equipment.
	Upgrades to computer software.
	Rent.
	Service charges.
	Utility costs.
	Insurance.
	Maintenance.
	Security.
	Training.
	Catering.
	Transport.
	Cash flow.
	(*Note*: some of these costs may be fixed, some may be variable – for example with volume of business.)

As mentioned earlier, a spreadsheet can be very useful in building up a cost model. Indeed, given the timetable for most bids it is hard to see how any other method would be able to support the costing and pricing calculations that would be needed. Some companies have their own models, and if they are available then use them. If they are not, then Figure 13.2 shows the layout (though not the formulae) of a costing spreadsheet for use as a starting point.

| Bid Title | | BS-NB Procurement | | Date 25/7/05 | | Bid Manager | David Nickson |
| | | | | | | Sales Manager | A Fox |

	October	November	December	Year One	Year Two	Year Three	Year Four	Total
Set-up costs								
Site manager	£1 000	£1 000	£1 200					£3 200
Installation engineer	£0	£2 000	£1 500					£3 500
Equipment	£10 000	£35 000	£8 000					£53 000
Delivery	£350	£500	£230					£1 080
Total	£11 350	£38 500	£10 930					£60 780

Operating costs	October	November	December	Year One	Year Two	Year Three	Year Four	Total
Helpdesk				£25 000	£26 000	£29 000	£30 000	£110 000
Security staff				£18 000	£18 000	£18 500	£19 000	£73 500
Maintenance				£12 000	£12 000	£12 000	£14 000	£50 000
Catering				£2 000	£2 000	£2 000	£3 000	£9 000
Upgrades				£0	£10 000	£1 200	£5 000	£16 200
Operators				£15 000	£15 000	£16 000	£16 000	£62 000
Site manager				£1 500	£1 600	£1 700	£1 775	£6 575
Installation engineer				£0	£1 500	£450	£1 500	£3 450
Delivery								£0
Total				£73 500	£86 100	£80 850	£90 275	£330 725

Note: maintenance quote fixed for first-three years.

Figure 13.2 *Layout of a costing spreadsheet*

> *Note.* Many costs will need to be estimated. The Bid Manager should make a point of challenging all cost estimates – those producing them should be able to offer a credible justification. If they cannot, then the risk associated with the price must be increased for any qualification process.

Pricing

Although the Bid Manager's role will not normally include the ownership of pricing, there will inevitably be considerable involvement in the pricing process. As with costing, there will be a substantial amount of work involved in this. Costing is essentially a matter of identifying items and allocating costs to them, even where the resulting model is complex. However, pricing is more of a 'black art'; consider all the variables that may be involved: payment schedules, payment options such as leasing, deals to be made on taking on existing staff, loss leader options, discounts for quantity/length of contract, optional extras, discounts for bundling together different options, and so on. The list is endless, limited only by the imaginations of the sales and procurement specialists involved.

It is important to understand the difference between a mark-up and a margin. A mark-up is expressed as a percentage increase applied to a base *cost*. For example, 20 per cent mark-up on £1000 is £1200 – the simpler approach. A margin is expressed as a percentage of the *price*. For instance, 20 per cent margin on a *price* of £1000 indicates a base cost of £800.

This is equivalent to a mark-up of 25 per cent. A more extreme example is that a margin of 50 per cent (that sounds large, but not excessive) represents a mark-up of 100 per cent (which might sound like a rip-off).

The author knows of one case where confusing the two resulted in the submission of a price that was significantly higher than it should have been. The services supply elements had been calculated at a 30 per cent margin instead of a 30 per cent mark-up. The bid was rejected on price.

Similarly it may be desirable to look at pricing on a per user basis, a per site basis, with or without an allowance for inflation, allowances for risk sharing and so forth. Pricing is a subject in its own right and the information here is intended to give a flavour of where the complexities can occur.

However complicated it is, the starting point for any pricing model must be a complete understanding of the costs. The bid team is the source of this information and will need to be able to generate new costings to support sales in their pricing negotiations with the client. A spreadsheet can be used to advantage here (Figure 13.3). As a starting point a pricing extension to the cost-only model for the previous section is provided.

Bid Title	BS-NB Procurement		Date 25/7/05		Bid Manager	David Nickson
					Sales Manager	A Fox

	October	November	December	Year One	Year Two	Year Three	Year Four	Total
Set-up costs								
Site manager	£1 000	£1 000	£1 200					£3 200
Installation engineer	£0	£2 000	£1 500					£3 500
Equipment	£10 000	£35 000	£8 000					£53 000
Delivery	£350	£500	£230					£1 080
Total	£11 350	£38 500	£10 930					£60 780

Operating costs	October	November	December	Year One	Year Two	Year Three	Year Four	Total
Helpdesk				£25 000	£26 000	£29 000	£30 000	£110 000
Security staff				£18 000	£18 000	£185 000	£19 000	£73 500
Maintenance				£12 000	£12 000	£12 000	£14 000	£50 000
Catering				£2 000	£2 000	£2 000	£3 000	£9 000
Upgrades				£0	£10 000	£1 200	£5 000	£16 200
Operators				£15 000	£15 000	£16 000	£16 000	£62 000
Site manager				£1 500	£1 600	£1 700	£1 775	£6 575
Installation engineer				£0	£1 500	£450	£1 500	£3 450
Delivery								£0
Total				£73 500	£86 100	£80 850	£90 275	£330 725

Revenue	October	November	December	Year One	Year Two	Year Three	Year Four	Total
Start-up fee	£0	£0	£15 000					£15 000
Service charge			£0	£100 000	£110 000	£115 000	£120 000	£445 000
Total	£0	£0	£15 000	£100 000	£110 000	£115 000	£120 000	£460 000
Costs	£11 350	£38 500	£10 930	£73 500	£86 100	£80 850	£90 275	£391 505
Profit/loss	–£11 350	–£38 500	£4 070	£26 500	£23 900	£34 150	£29 725	£68 495

Figure 13.3   *Layout of a pricing spreadsheet*

CASE STUDY

SITUATION

NB Ltd, a small engineering company, were bidding to BS plc, a supplier of automated warehouse equipment, for specialist machine tools. NB had a long-standing relationship with BS, but as a supplier of finished goods rather than machine tools, which was a new part of the business that had resulted from a takeover. They were asked to bid because of the relationship, even though they had no track record of supplying such equipment to BS. NB's sales staff were used to negotiating contracts for the bulk supply of similar items, for example adjustable shelf brackets. A typical sale might be for 5000 pairs of brackets at £20 each. The sales job was almost entirely concerned with negotiating payment terms, delivery dates and discounts for prompt payment. The new business was for one-off items of complex equipment designed to do a very specific job. This required technical knowledge so it was decided to get the engineering manager to handle this particular sale.

PROBLEM

The engineering manager, together with two support staff, put together a bid in conjunction with the sales manager, who was to assist with negotiating the final deal. Up until recently NB Ltd had only supplied finished goods; the venture into supplying specialist machine tools was a new one. Consequently, the company had limited experience in this type of sale and was happy to treat this as a learning exercise for all concerned. The bid team put the bid document together as a response to an ITT issued by BS plc. They had not done this sort of thing before but went about answering all the points as precisely and accurately as possible. Most of the questions related to performance and technical capability of the machinery to be supplied, training, how it would be supported and so on.

OUTCOME

NB Ltd did not win the contract to supply the machine tools. They were thanked for their bid but as this was a commercial procurement, and they did not ask, there was no debrief meeting so they were not immediately told why they lost. However, the closeness of the relationship between the NB sales manager and the procurement executive at BS plc led to the story coming out over a drink. The bid document had answered the questions in the ITT thoroughly. However, the questions had been answered without any attempt to sell the NB equipment.

LESSON LEARNT

NB decided to send two of their engineers on a sales awareness course so that they would be better able to support a sales exercise in the future. It was intended to make sales awareness part of the induction programme for all new staff who would come into contact with clients directly or who would need to support sales as part of the job.

Checklist

Item	Description	Completed?
Qualification	Is there a qualification methodology? Does it have well-defined evaluation criteria? Are the bid approval decision makers identified? What is the process? What documentation is required? Is it available? (e.g. risk register, bid brief, copy of client documents, costing, pricing, etc.)	
SWOT	Strengths identified? Weaknesses identified? Competition evaluated?	
Costing	Are all one-off costs defined? Are all recurrent costs defined? Cash flow charges? Inflation allowances? VAT?	
Pricing	Are all costs identified? Payment schedule defined? Payment options identified (leasing etc.)? Discounts? Optional items? Bundling price reductions? Premature termination fees? Loss leader? VAT?	

Appendix: Bid Brief Template

BID BRIEF

for

Client Name/Procurement

Reference Numbers

Version *1.0*

NN/MMM/YY

Authors
ANO

©   ABC, 2002

Commercial-in-Confidence

INSTRUCTIONS FOR USE:

This template provides a generic structure for a Bid Brief for ABC use when responding to large/formal proposals. Bid Managers should feel free to edit the document to suit their individual bid but should maintain the same structure and intellectual content. Anything in italics needs to be edited (or, in the case of these instructions, removed) to fit requirements of the bid. The size of the Brief will increase/decrease to suit the individual bid.

<u>**CONTENTS**</u>   **Page No.**

Commercial-in-Confidence

1   INTRODUCTION

1.1   Purpose and Scope

This Bid Brief document is to provide the team members preparing the response to the *Customer procurement/nnnn* with a clear brief on what is required, to produce a winning bid response document. This document will provide a general background on the Client. The document will be issued a number of times based on information obtained to date.

This document and the information produced for the customer response document is valuable information for our competitors. It is therefore important that team members safeguard this information throughout the bid production process. All documents associated with this bid are to be classified as 'Commercial in Confidence'.

1.2   Change Summary

Version 1.0   First Issue

1.3   Reference Material

Other related documents e.g. relevant sales plan etc.

2　　THE BID ENVIRONMENT

2.1　　The Client's Business

Description of the customer's business and basic statistics such as number of staff, turnover, market/market share, perceived strategic direction. Relevant background to the procurement.

2.2　　ABC and the Client Position

Existing relationship (if any) between ABC and Client. Names of key customer contacts/their role, projects/services delivered in the past and estimate of their success/failure rating. How the scope of any existing supply relates to the new procurement.

2.3　　Procurement Scope

A description of the scope and value of the procurement, broken down (estimates if necessary) in terms of products/service/management delivery. Scope the whole project/delivery and relate it to ABC's ability to deliver/necessity to use third parties.

2.4　　Significant Dates in the Procurement Process

Key dates in procurement, e.g. when OR/ITT due, when drafts are needed, when proposal has to be delivered to client, BAFO, award of contract, etc.

3   APPROACH

3.1   The Win Strategy

How ABC expects to win the business. This should be a short description and it is here to focus attention on what is relevant to this Client.

3.1.1   Evaluation Criteria

Where known (if not, why not!) or as guessed.

Typically things like:

> *Company profile*
> *Sales service*
> *Implementation service quality*
> *Support service quality*
> *Warranty provision*
> *Product quality*
> *Price control mechanisms*
> *Product range*
> *Compliance with contractual and procurement requirements*
> *Price/costs of products and services*

3.1.2 Competitors

Known, and guessed, competitors for business. Possibly and assessment of their strengths and weaknesses re: this procurement.

3.2   Sales Themes

The key themes for the bid – to ensure that all writers of copy are following a common line.

Typically such things as: ABC as a safe choice based on understanding of the business, proven track record of delivery, ability to supply products/services needed, Implementation expertise, Enterprise experience, Training, Reference sites.

4   THE PROPOSAL DEVELOPMENT METHODOLOGY

4.1   Objective

What the objective of doing the proposal is

For example –

To respond to the OR and achieve the shortlist of suppliers by:

- *fully complying with all Mandatory requirements;*
- *complying with all Desirable Requirements at competitively priced options;*
- *submitting a bid that demonstrates ABC's Strengths;*
- *demonstrate within the response that ABC is the best company to deliver the requirements.*

4.2   Methodology

Introduction

Contributions to the bid document will come from *ABC, strategic projects, sales, services, third parties etc., etc., and other proposals* for which we have been shortlisted. This will be collated and edited by a Bid Manager.

To create a seamless and consistent document it is essential that all contributors follow the same methodology defined below:

- *Schedule the development and production of the bid*
- *Define the responsibilities for all members of the team*
- *Make the responsibilities visible to all members of the team*
- *Ensure that all the document sections are allocated to people with the relevant skills*
- *Describe the structure and format of the bid*
- *Formal quality reviews of the document*
- *Establish the standards for the document consistency of grammar, terminology, layout*
- *Establish the identified Sales theme consistently throughout the document*

Optional figure showing understanding of requirement.

4.3   Quality Control

Introduction

The prime objective is to build selling quality, accuracy into the bid document so that the customer will have no doubt as to *ABC*'s ability and capabilities to deliver the customer requirements. A summary of the purpose and quality objectives follows:

Bid Brief Document

The issue of this Brief will define the general structure of the bid, the team responsibilities and the general methodology to be used. The Bid Brief is a living document for the period of the Bid production process. The document will be controlled by the Bid Manager.

Draft Bid Document

The first draft is to be produced to review and ensure that the technical outline follows the identified themes and to initially assess progress against the bid production timescales. The Bid Manager will nominate the Core Bid team members to conduct this review.

Red Team Review

The Red Team's primary objective is:

- to appraise the technical and commercial risk;

- to formally review and appraise the technical and commercial compliance to the customer's OR and evaluation criteria;

- to review the selling ability as a logical persuasive document which puts forward a sound, justified and coherent case why the customer should purchase from ABC plc.

Quality Check

The Quality Check will assess the progress and quality of the document production against the standards as well as Red Team corrections/emphasis.

Book Check

The Book Check will ensure that each copy of the Bid document is complete in all respects down to the page level.

5   THE BID PROPOSAL PLAN

5.1   The Bid Team Organization

Introduction

To implement the methodology described in the Bid Team Organization has been designed to meet the identified work areas and resource requirements.

Bid Manager	*ANO*
Business Manager	*ANO*
Bid Production Manager	*ANO*
Technical Manager	*ANO*
Commercial	*ANO*
Project Manager Designate	*ANO*
Technical Consultant Demonstrations	*ANO*
Technical Researchers	*ANO*
Admin/Sect Support	*ANO*

5.2   Bid Production Organization Chart

This is optional, but helpful.

Bid Team Organization

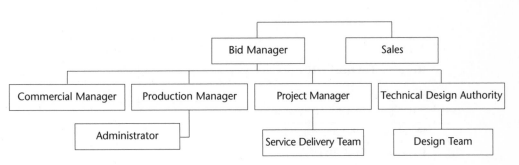

BID BRIEF TEMPLATE
Version 1.0

Commercial-in-Confidence

5.3   Bid Production Milestone Plan

Key dates from the plan.

To be revised / developed by the Bid Manager

***e.g.* Bid Production Milestones**

Activity	Date
Receive Formal OR	
Issue Bid Brief	
Bid Team Meeting & Review	
Determine OR Queries	
Produce First Draft	
Develop Pricing	
Review First Draft	
Produce Red Team Draft	
Red Team Review	
Final Proposal Revision	
Quality Check	
Proposal Sign-Off	
Production and Book Check	
Deliver Bid to Customer	

ANNEX A – THE BID STRUCTURE, THEMES AND RESPONSIBILITIES

A.1   Proposal Structure/Themes

Note: It is vital that all authors read the sections (*reference here*) of the Client's requirement which specifies what they want in each chapter, this is not reproduced here to keep the document short.

For example:

Chapter 1   Management Summary

Chapter Manager A Seller
Themes: Service, Catalogue Expertise, Compliancy, Delivery Expertise and References.

Chapter 2   Introduction

Chapter Manager   A Seller
Themes: Demonstrate Understanding of Requirement, Benefits of Strengths of Services/Training/Implementation, Catalogue Management skills.

Note: For larger bids you may choose to use the 'frame' pro forma at chapter, section, sub-section level as appropriate (see overleaf for example/template).

Commercial-in-Confidence

Chapter Title	Bid Name	Chapter Manager
Management Summary	Example Bid Brief	David Nickson

Section: 1 – Introduction	**Target Word Count:** 200
Section Author: David Nickson	**Sub Section Author:** n/a

Sales Themes

Company as partner not supplier vs customer.

Established, good, working relationship from previous business.

Market leader.

Track record.

Reference sites.

Low risk technical solution.

Easily measurable performance gains.

Synopsis (Optional)

Introduces structure of the management summary and underlines the key sales themes in brief before setting scene for the benefits to be gained in detail.

Contributors: n/a

First Draft By:	Red Team Draft by:	Proof by:	Publication on:
03/Aug/05	11/Aug/05	17/Aug/05	19/Aug/05

A.2   Responsibility Matrix

(Not always necessary but helpful for larger bids).

This specifies the source of information for the proposal. The Information Providers are provisional at this stage, but if you think it's not you then say ASAP. In some cases the Information Provider will delegate the work. When individuals have been identified to replace high level IPs the matrix will be updated and individuals will be given fresh copies. This table identifies who is responsible for the information and when it is required.

The references are to the customer's requirement document *(ref)* and to the place they will go in the skeleton proposal to complete it.

Identified IPs are:

Name	Information required/reference

Use this format where there are specific mandatory/desirable requirements etc.

A.1   Mandatory Requirements

Note: The 1st Draft/Red Team Draft Columns will be used for bid progress management.

Customer Reference	Proposal Reference	Information Provider	1st Draft Deadline nn.mm.y	Red Team Deadline nn.mm.y
nnn	*mmmm*	*ANO*		

A.2   Desirable Requirements

O.R. Reference	Proposal Reference	Information Provider	1st Draft Deadline nn.mm.y	Red Team Deadline nn.mm.y
nnn	*mmmm*	*ANO*		

Annex B – PROPOSAL DEVELOPMENT STANDARDS

Edit the following to suit.

<u>Text and Artwork Standards</u>

- The format and layout of the document will be established by the Bid Manager and is not an issue for contributors.
- The complete Bid Document will be produced using Microsoft Word™ (version Office XP).
- Contributors creating paragraphs of text should ensure that Word™ 6 files are placed on 3.5" floppy disks or sent via email.
- Authors should retain copies of all document files submitted to the Central Publication PC for incorporation in the Bid proposal document on their own PCs and on floppy disk (back-up).
- All files produced by a spreadsheet application must be able to be fully interpreted by the Microsoft EXCEL™ spreadsheet.

<u>Terminology and Grammar</u>

Spelling

English spelling is used throughout. The spell checker must always be used especially before major reviews and for the final document run.

Note the spelling conventions and use of upper or lower case as shown below:

MS-DOS
Intel
WAN and LAN
PC
PCs (as in plural) and PC's (as in the possessive case 'the PC's hard disk capacity is')
disk (not disc)
ABC is singular!
on-line
use on-site and off-site
use e.g. and i.e.
use the Client.

Glossary

Although every attempt has been made to explain any special terms as they are introduced, some may have been missed. Also it is felt that for any bid a glossary of terms is always of help to the reader. The aim of this book is to get the reader to buy into managing bids in a more effective way, so in part this book is a bid itself. So, here is the glossary of phrases, acronyms and abbreviations used in this book. There is no prize for spotting any that have been left out, but feel free to write them in yourself at the end.

Abbreviation	Compressed form of word or phrase with the intention of saving space. For instance 'i/c' instead of in charge. BM instead of Bid Manager.
Acronym	Real or artificial word formed by taking initials from phrase with the intention of providing something memorable, for example, SMART (simple, measurable, achievable, realistic, timetable).
BAFO	Best And Final Offer – an example of an acronym.
Bid brief	Collection of useful information relating to a bid for use as a briefing and control document. Sometimes called a bid directory or bid bible.
BM	Bid Manager.
BMP	Derived from 'bitmap' this is a non-compressed (large) file format for storing pictures.
Cash flow	Difference between moneys in and out within a fixed time period.
Clip art	Ready-made pictures, images and cartoons for use in documents and presentations. These are typically non-copyright and provided in conjunction with an Office Suite or DTP application.
Controlled document	A document that is subject to formal change control and which may also have a limited circulation that may have to be signed for.
Database	Collection of information, usually stored on a computer; also used to denote a computer application that manages data.
Delegation	Effectively, passing a task to another member of the team.
Deliverables	Anything that the project is required to produce in order to be completed.
DTP	Desktop publishing.
Due diligence	The process of ensuring that all people bidding for/making a purchase are entitled to ask, and have answered, all reasonable questions concerning material facts affecting the contract.
Email	Electronic mail.
FOC	Free of charge.
Gantt chart	Bar chart linking tasks in sequence; developed in the nineteenth century by Henry Gant.

Internet	Public access information distribution system, often used to support email and WWW transmission.
Intranet	Internet-like information distribution system only accessible from within an organization.
IT	Information technology.
ITN	Invitation to negotiate.
ITT	Invitation to tender.
JPEG	Compressed file format for storing pictures.
MAC	Shortened from Macintosh. Now a generic term for Apple range of personal computers.
Margin	The percentage of the price of the project that represents profit.
Mark-up	A percentage or fraction of the estimated cost of a project added to the cost to produce a price. (Margin is not the same as price.)
Methodology	Collection of processes, measures and controls used for managing tasks. Methodologies exist for project management, risk management, sales management and so on.
MPEG	JPEG for moving pictures. Compressed format for video.
MS	Microsoft – software supplier.
Negotiable item	Something that you wish to trade with/for, for example, the price, access to resources.
Office suite	Collection of computer programs typically including word processing, spreadsheet, presentation and possibly database components.
OGC	Office of Government Commerce. Often involved in overseeing government procurements that include computers and telecommunications (took over from the CCTA).
OJEC	*Official Journal of the European Community.*
OR	Organizational requirement.
Organization chart	A diagram showing who reports to whom, who does what, etc.
PC	Personal computer – implies systems derived from original IBM design.
PDF	Postscript definition file – a portable documents format for Internet and publishing use. This is an Adobe ™ product.
PERT chart	Project Evaluation and Review Tool – a network diagram showing how tasks are linked together; developed in the 1960s by Lockheed Aircraft Corporation for the Polaris Missile project.
PFI	Private Finance Initiative. Government procurement method.
PPP	Public Private Partnership. Government procurement model.
Prime contractor	Organization with overall responsibility for delivering a project.
PRINCE	A project development system (projects in a controlled environment).
QA	Quality assurance.
Quality control	Attempt to ensure that deliverables are produced to a consistent standard.
Red team	Independent team whose purpose is to review a bid.
RFI	Request for information.
RFP	Request for proposal.

RFQ	Request for quotation.
RI	Readibility index.
Risk	A threat to all, or part, of the project's viability/cost/timescale. Usually expressed in terms of impact and probability.
Risk register	A record of identified project risks.
Spreadsheet	Computer-based tool very useful for costing and pricing exercises.
Style Guide	Collection of information that defines the look and feel of a document/web site and so on.
Subcontractor	Organization/person working for a prime contractor.
SWOT	Strengths, weaknesses, opportunities, threats.
TACs	Terms and conditions for a contract.
Task	Identified work to be done by person/team.
Team working	Interactive way of working involving a group of people with common objectives.
Third party	Organization/person outside of the project team.
TUPE	Transfer of Undertakings (Protection of Employment).
USP	Unique selling point.
WBS	Work breakdown structure – term used in project management for showing how work is split up within a project.
Web site	Site on the Internet/WWW presenting information in page format. May include words, pictures, audio, video and so on.
WMF	Windows Meta File. A bit-mapped graphic file format for storing pictures, images, cartoons, and so on.
WP/word processor	Text manipulation application – vital for producing bid documents. A component of all office suites.
WWW	World Wide Web – Internet page-based sources of information.

Additional Reading

The following books have been found helpful by the author and would provide additional, and more in-depth, information for the reader.

John Adair, *Effective Time Management: How to Save Time and Spend it Wisely*, London: Pan Books, 1988.

R. Meredith Belbin, *Management Teams: Why They Succeed or Fail*, Oxford: Butterworth-Heinemann, 1996.

Chris Churchouse and Jane Churchouse, *Managing Projects*, Aldershot: Gower, 1999.

Martin Cutts, *The Plain English Guide*, Oxford: Oxford University Press, 1995.

Gavin Kennedy, *Everything is Negotiable*, London: Random House, 1997.

David Nickson and Suzy Siddons, *Managing Projects*, Oxford: Butterworth-Heinemann, 1998.

Suzy Siddons, *Presentations Skills*, London: Chartered Institute of Personnel Development, 1999.

Index